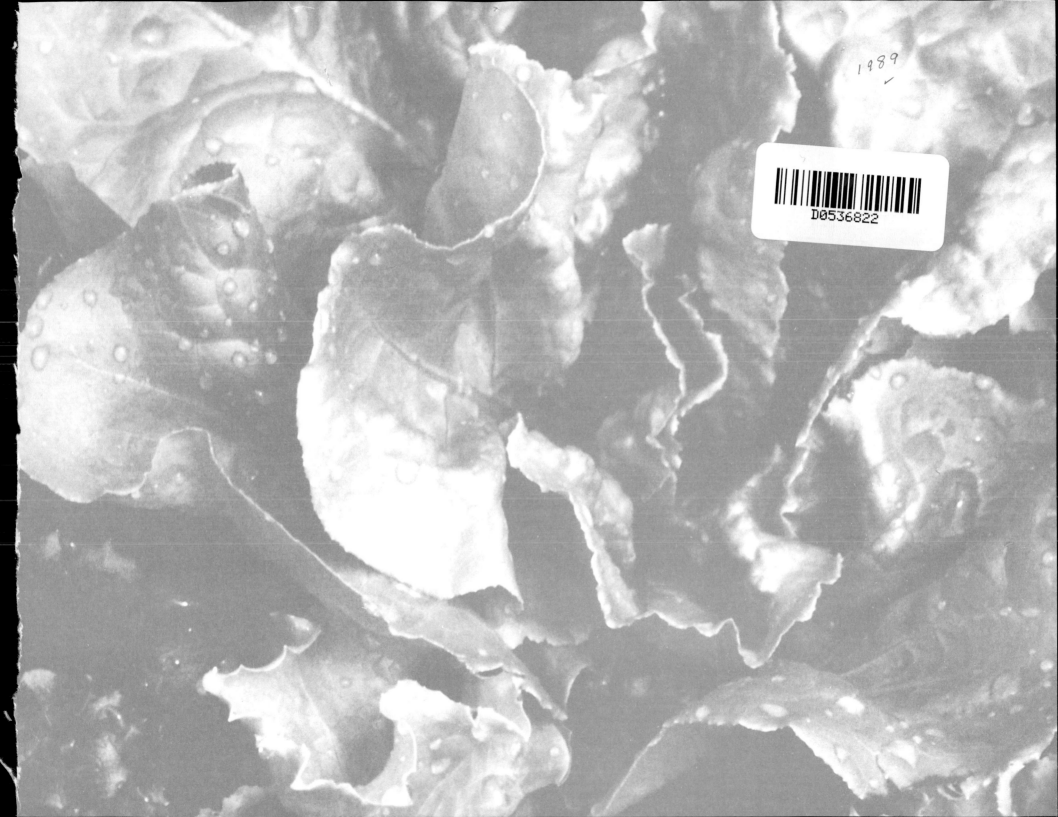

1989

CHRISTOPHER IDONE'S SALAD DAYS

CHRISTOPHER IDONE'S
SALAD DAYS

WINE SUGGESTIONS BY YVES-ANDRÉ ISTEL

CALORIE COUNTS BY PATRICIA F. MESSING, M.S.

RANDOM HOUSE NEW YORK

Oh, green and glorious! Oh, herbaceous treat!
'Twould tempt the dying anchorite to eat;
Back to the world he'd turn his fleeting soul,
And plunge his fingers in the salad bowl!
Serenely full, the epicure would say,
'Fate cannot harm me, I have dined today.'
—Reverend Sydney Smith

Library of Congress Cataloging-in-Publication Data

Idone, Christopher.

Christopher Idone's salad days.

Includes index.
1. Salads. I. Title. II. Title: Salad days.
TX740.I36   1989   641.8'3   86-29750
ISBN 0-394-56584-3

Manufactured in Singapore
98765432

ACKNOWLEDGEMENTS

To the friends who chopped, tasted, critiqued and adjusted the random rolling tomato, I especially want to thank Cheryl Merser and Christine and Yves-André Istel for their support and the pleasure of their company. To Rico Puhlmann who encouraged me to photograph my own work and the general joy of having working moments with Rena Coyle, Mardee Haidin Regan and Rebecca Atwater; and Pat Messing for supplying calorie counts— sometimes higher than I wanted.

I also want to thank those friends who allowed me to invade their kitchens and gardens—and those there to cheer me on—Ann Johnson, Lena Tabori, Eugenie Voorhees, Elizabeth Esteve, Joachim Esteve, Jason Epstein, and Paige and David Peterson.

I also wish to thank Shepherd Ogden for his catalogs, seeds, herbs and sharing his knowledge of the salad garden—all from the Cook's Garden in Londonderry, Vermont. Also Gary Feldman at Bink and Bink in New York City and Windfall Farms for supplying mesclun; and John Haessler at the Seafood Shop in Wainscott.

And to Robert Scudellari for his encouragement and unerring eye and to Carol Schneider at Random House for her enthusiastic help, my thanks again.   —Christopher Idone

CONTENTS

CONTENTS

No one documented the first salad, but whoever first mixed shreds of fresh lettuce with a handful of wild herbs, or buds, or knots of fiddleheads, or wild grasses, and tossed them together with salt, some acidy wine, and a touch of fruity olive oil, was on to a good thing. This first salad probably originated in ancient Greece or Rome, and the simple and oddly wondrous dressing of acid and natural oil they used then has served us well ever since.

Our word "salad" comes from the Latin *herba salata*, "salted greens," and the Italians call their salads *insalata* today. This simple mixture is often served up with a loaf of bread, a bottle of wine, and perhaps a little dish of herbed olives and a plate of cheese to make a complete meal. The ancient Spartans ate cresses, gathered from streams in early spring, with bread. The French serve what is known as a "classic" salad—a few tender, green leaves tossed with vinaigrette—after the main meal, or sometimes on the side. And quite often in American homes and restaurants a salad will not end, or even accompany, a meal, but rather introduce it. A buttered slice of crusty bread with a filling of peppery, juicy leaves and stems of watercress is more filling than a one-bite tea sandwich, and reminds me of an equally appealing French favorite: a buttered slice of baguette heaped with sliced radishes sprinkled with salt. In effect—a salad sandwich! Perhaps there aren't any hard and fast rules about salads after all.

There are many different sorts of salads after the simple green salad. Some are "composed" (*salades composées*) and incorporate many ingredients, artfully arranged. They are usually served with two or more dressings, maybe a vinaigrette and a herb mayonnaise. Elaborate salads, which first began to appear on tables in eighteenth-century England, were elevated to a new luxury in France by Escoffier, who included extravagant ingredients such as boned quail breasts, truffles, crayfish, and foie gras. And ornate aspic salads such as *boeuf en gelée* and molded vegetable mosaics have long been an elegant part of the haute cuisine repertoire.

Salads need not be restricted to a certain form. Any plant that can be eaten raw, or any that can be cooked and eaten cold, can make up a salad. No matter what greens you choose, the first consideration should always be freshness. Many vegetables can be revived with cooking, and many a blemished carrot or tired onion is fine in a stew, but just won't do for a salad. The ingredients for a salad must be fresh. And, if I were you, I'd save the wilted and rusted leaves for the rabbits.

The best things in life have short seasons. Tomatoes are best in August and September, just as radishes taste best in early spring. In fact, just about everything nature gives us has a moment when it is perfection. And that is what you seek and should remember when making a salad.

Salads have changed tremendously in less than a decade. Today, they are full of invention and apt to include whatever we may plant in our own gardens or find fresh at the market. The salad is considered the new meal. Meats, fowl, and fish are bedded on a mess of greens with julienned vegetables and whatever else may strike the fancy of the cook. Salads appeal to the calorie-conscious, and the payoff is sensible nutrition with mouth-watering good food on the plate.

We start craving summer salads by the end of winter, when our hankering for greens is profound. We notice people trudging along the highways in search of dandelions, lamb's quarters, burdock, wild leeks, violets, and cress. We reach down to pick a slip of wild onion grass, or nip a fiddlehead fern to crunch, fresh and raw, wanting, by pure instinct, to taste the luscious newness. As summer approaches we lighten our diets, and are less inclined to spend long hours preparing food. Friends drop in unannounced, or bring an extra guest or two at lunchtime. And though the invitation may have been for only two instead of three, we still have to serve up a lunch of some sort, whether we want to or not! Summer is a time for impromptu entertaining, and the simplest solution is the salad.

These situations are precisely why, during hot months, I cook extra fish or meat, save vegetables, and prepare greens ahead of time. If you start keeping a summer larder stocked, all of your lunches can be simple, light, and quick to make. Keep radishes trimmed, cleaned, and packed in ice water, and they will stay crisp. Store a few day's supply of scallions, a variety of olives, and unshelled hard-cooked eggs in the refrigerator; keep your shelves stocked with olive, peanut, and vegetable oils, an array of vinegars, mustards, anchovies, tuna fish, garlic, and capers, and have a tub of tended herbs close to the kitchen door. Dinner, too, can be a salad—as filling a main course as you could want. If you doubt me, try the Warm Chicken and Mango Salad or Lime-Marinated Swordfish and Squash Salad and finish the meal with a rich dessert or fruit.

Summer's delights are not winter's pleasures. From early fall until the first frost, gardens and markets burst with the last gasp of summer's abundance. Tomatoes still have that wonderful, sweet, acid, juicy taste; all varieties of vegetables are there for the choosing—lettuces of every kind, beans of every shape and color, and a profusion of herbs that are beginning to flower or already have, now to be brought indoors or left to wither and die. At the same time reminders of winter's harvest to come begin to weave through this cornucopia—parsnips; salsify; cabbages, red, green, and sweetly crinkled Savoy; cauliflowers, purple and white; wild rice; cranberries; horseradish; beets; fennel; and artichokes.

Winter is not a sad time for the salad lover. The inventive Italians slice the white stalk of the sweet anise-flavored fennel as thin as paper and toss it with fruity olive oil, ground black pepper, and then shave sheets of Parmesan on top. They do the same with baby artichokes when the hearts and inner lavender thistles are as tender as butter. And then there are the lettuces and chicories. It used to be that the poor shopper was doomed to a winter salad diet of supermarket bunches of leathery romaine, heads of chicory big enough to feed a family of twelve, and, of course, the perennial Iceberg. (I don't condemn Iceberg. It is mostly made of water, and its nutritional value is almost nil, but it is durable, it has a nice crunch, and when shredded, it is delicious with a hamburger, a BLT, or as the base for a crab salad with Louis dressing.) Today, we can pick through the greengrocer's array of romaines and find sweet and tender Kentucky limestone (Bibb) or Sucrine (even smaller than Bibb) or bronzing *Rouge d'Hiver.* The crisphead lettuces like Iceberg are being replaced by *Reine* and *Tête de Glaces* and the burnished red Grenoble. Silky ivory stalks of Belgian endive are available throughout the country, and the frizzy chicory is arriving at markets, blanched and curled to creamy perfection. And we have, at no small cost, I might add, tender sweet clusters of *mâche.* To all this we add fish, meat, fowl, or smoked game and spike our salads with colorful exotica such as cactus pears, tamarillos, carambolas, Jerusalem artichokes, and pummelos from as far away as Brazil, New Zealand, and Japan. No, winter is not a hardship. The salad becomes more substantial, more often than not warm, but remains as quick and easy as summer's best.

Unlike some meals that demand elaborate preparation, most of the recipes in this book are easy to make and many can be assembled at the last minute. Though a few require a bit of planning, others are pulled together from leftovers embellished with greens, herbs, and flowers. These salads are meant to be casual plates of food that show off our ingenuity rather than our expertise as cooks. They are the harvest of the four seasons—little surprises I have cooked up over the years, in pleasant idle hours and harried moments both. I hope they enable you to enjoy the little time you must spend in the kitchen, and the time you'll save for other pleasures.

Lettuces are grown all over the world: in the cloudy atmosphere of English gardens and on valley farms of alpine Italy; on the high-production farms of California, and along the steep slopes of the Rockies (where they are harvested in a very short season and chicly called "tundra greens"). Every civilization has its own lettuce lore. The ancient Egyptians used the milky juice from the stalks as an aphrodisiac and some considered it a non-habit-forming tranquilizer, similar to opium. The English, on the other hand, thought that lettuces suppressed sexual appetite. The Romans maintained that lettuce prevented hangovers if eaten after the wine was drunk, and until recently drinking wine with salad continued to raise eyebrows. Medieval pharmaceutical literature refers to wafers made from the dried juices of lettuce to be prescribed for insomniacs, the wounded, and those going under the knife.

What is more American today than a crisp salad? American colonists rarely ate greens; theirs was a steady diet of beans, pork, and maize. By the early 1880s, however, American seed catalogues offered a good dozen lettuce varieties and farm hothouses surrounding Boston were supplying greens even during the cold winters. Today there are hundreds of lettuces to choose from, with wonderful names like Black Seeded Simpson, Bibb (the first American fancy lettuce), Kwiek (planted in early spring), Kloek (planted in late fall), May King, Ice Queen, Green Ice, and plain old Iceberg.

Lettuces are a garden unto themselves. Some flower like roses, some stand tall and firm, while others grow frizzled and curly. All are colorfully tinted, from the palest green to emerald, from bronze to ruby. There are creamy yellow lettuces and others that are variegated and tinged with green or red or bronze. Some are so tender that they melt like butter in your mouth, some are crunchy and crisp, and still others are firm and almost rough on the tongue. Lettuces fall into four categories: loose-leaf, butterhead, crisphead and Cos (also known as romaine).

Loose-leaf lettuces are nonheading and their leaves grow curly, frilly, or in rosettes. They are light green in color, with some strains tinged with bronze or red. They are popular varieties in home gardens and at local farm markets. These slightly crisp lettuces, with their pale to delicate flavors, wilt quickly and are best eaten soon after picking (or purchasing). Loose-leaf lettuces mature most quickly of all. Names that will be familiar to you when you buy or plant them include the Black Seeded Simpson, green and red Salad Bowl, Oak Leaf (both green and red), and Ruby. Loose-leaf lettuces are pretty, ornamental enough to use for borders in flower gardens, and wonderful as potted plants for the sunny city terrace or kitchen window. The leaves can be picked as they mature, and so the plant will produce for as long as a month. A single head can fill the salad bowl, and the small leaves from the rosettes make delicate additions to pretty salads.

Butterhead are known as "hearting" lettuces because the smallest, innermost leaves are densely packed; the hearts are tender with soft, sweet, flappy leaflets. Bibb, also known as Kentucky limestone (or just "limestone"), and the Dark Green Boston and White Boston are the best known of the butterhead group. In winter, the Boston strains are grown in local greenhouses. The hydroponically-grown Boston and Bibbs appear at markets in wintertime as well. Four Seasons—a beautiful green-leafed lettuce tinged with rich cranberry red—originated in France and has become a restaurant and cultivators' favorite here. Kwiek and Kloek are butterheads, too. Because the outer leaves of butterheads are tender and bruise easily, produce markets often appear to be selling half a head of lettuce—as blemished leaves are discarded, the vegetables are peeled down almost to the buttery hearts. Like loose-leaf varieties, butterheads combine well with sturdier leaf lettuces; they also make a nice foil for watercress. They are excellent with creamy vinaigrettes, especially those flavored with delicate herbs such as tarragon or chervil, and a hint of mustard.

Crisphead lettuces instantly bring to mind the tasteless king of them all: Iceberg. This variety is known for its tight, dense head and its pale silvery green color. Iceberg lettuce is more than 90 percent water. In defense of this most common of lettuces, it must be said that it keeps very well. And a big chunk of

Iceberg with a piece or two of cottony tomato, all drowned in creamy blue cheese dressing, can be the stuff of memories. Another crisphead variety of note is *Tête de Glaces,* from Belgium, which occasionally appears in our markets and seed catalogues; it, too, is chunky, with a crisp texture and nutty flavor.

Cos, or romaine, derives its name from the Greek island of Kos. The Romans brought it home with them and carried it as far as the papal gardens of Avignon. Thus it is known in France (and more commonly here) as "romaine." Little Gem or Sugar Cos is a dwarf variety; growth stops at six inches. This lettuce with its crispy, tasty heart stands up well when tossed in the salad bowl (as do all Cos types) and takes well to pungent cheese dressings like Roquefort and other blues—and a Caesar Salad could not be made without it.

Mesclun is a leafy mix of salad plants and herbs once picked wild from the Alpine regions of Italy, France, and Switzerland. These greens are eaten during the early spring and into the early summer months and appear regularly on the menus of restaurants and homes where Provençal cooking is a way of life. Small specialty farms on both the East and West coasts grow these luxurious combinations in small quantities.

Chicory is a green that has many cousins. There is wild chicory, similar to dandelion, that is gathered by the roadside, and there's the wild variety cultivated especially for the Italian produce markets. There is witloof chicory grown to make the coffee-like beverage, and there is silky, gossamer endive, a tight-leafed and creamy stalk. Radicchio is ever gaining in popularity among cooks and restaurant chefs;

anyone who needs to decorate a plate has replaced the tried and not-too-true carrot curl with a little red radicchio leaf. There are dozens of Italian varieties, all of which turn their lusty red colors only after the first frost—radicchio is truly a winter lettuce. The frizzy chicory (what the French call *frisée*) is one of the more beautiful varieties—pale green outer leaves edging a white center. Except for the Italian red chicories, most varieties are "blanched," of creamy color and a less sharp flavor.

Bitter and small greens abound. Sorrel, rocket, and dandelion, in addition to turnip and mustard greens, are referred to as "bitter greens." Sorrel is tart and acid, lemony in flavor but tamer than wild sourgrass. The smaller stems and leaves should be mixed sparingly into salads, and the large leaves left for soups, purees, and sauces. Rocket, also known as arugula, is most often enjoyed as a cultivated plant, although wild varieties can be pleasant (among them sea rocket, with its salty taste). These greens, along with small greens such as purslane, are ancient plants; the wild varieties are the curse of American gardeners, while the French have domesticated them and use them extensively in exotic salads. Dandelion is a pungent leaf, which grows tougher and more bitter as spring rushes by; it is a delicious and vitamin-packed treat for a couple of months—and cheap. The little nugget-like buds can be fried and tossed into salads, and pulled golden petals can decorate the dish.

There are hundreds of varieties of cress, the most popular being "upland" or "field" cress (a form of watercress that grows in lazy, shallow streams) and "garden" or "English" cress (a miniature cress normally grown on dampened felt or paper towels, and popular as a tea sandwich ornament). Cress are peppery-flavored greens known for centuries as "poor man's pepper." They mix well with other greens and when served with a little olive oil, lemon juice, and salt and pepper, make by themselves a delicious end to a meal.

Many of these greens are available in markets throughout spring and summer; the wild varieties are best picked in spring before they flower. They are well suited to strong dressings heavily scented with garlic, and lend themselves to hot dressings and wilting.

Spinach is with us all year long. But we think of it as a winter green when the leaves are black-green and the surface bubbly and thickly rumpled. We serve it up with chopped hard-cooked egg, bacon bits, and croutons to disguise the lackluster of this plant. Smooth, pointed leaf spinach, a strain from Italy and France, has been introduced in many produce markets and seed catalogues. This spinach makes for better eating—especially when raw. The smooth-leafed variety holds up well on its own, and the tender stalks add a nice light crunch to a salad. The tougher stringy stems of other varieties should be removed. Spinach combines well with other crunchy raw vegetables such as sweet bell peppers and asparagus. For my taste, it is a green that shows off best when the dressing is hot and the greens wilted.

Swiss chard and beet tops both make for excellent salad eating. The large leaves are best served cooked or wilted, with hot dressings. The stems should be cut from the leaves and cooked until slightly tender. When the chard or beet leaves are 3- to 4-inches high, the stems can be served raw as well. Chard is rich and meaty with a tender texture. It is complimented by the addition of toasted nuts, hearty hard Italian cheeses, hard goat cheeses, and nut oils.

Lamb's lettuce, also known as corn salad, lamb's tongue, or *mâche,* is a perishable and delicate leaf. It grows wild or domesticated, and though available in spring and early summer, it is more often to be found in markets in late fall and winter. It is gathered, washed, and served in clusters, and deserves a light vinaigrette tamed with a fruit vinegar, preferably raspberry.

There are cabbages for every season. Round cabbages, white or red, are sturdier than the more delicate Chinese or Savoy varieties. The crunchy texture of cabbage is excellent for raw slaws, or blanched or stir-fried hot slaws.

Buying and Cleaning Salad Greens

Greens should appeal first to the eye. They should be crisp and free of spots and yellowing marks, and they should certainly not be limp. Greengrocers often spray or wash their lettuces for attractive presentation. If the greens are sold by the pound, give them a good shake or two, and save a few cents in water weight. Avoid oversize heads of lettuces and cresses and spinach with oversize stems, as they tend to be tough and chewy.

To store greens, I poke a few holes in a plastic bag and place the greens inside. It is important that air has room to circulate around the leaves. Store in the vegetable bin of the refrigerator. Do not keep them for more than a couple of days, as they wilt and tend to go bad quickly. To wash lettuce, remove the leaves, drop them in a large pot or sink full of cold water, and swish them around with your hand. Transfer to a colander and check to see if you've removed all of the grit, sand, or dirt from the leaves. If not, repeat the process. Drain in a colander and tear away the tough stems and any spotted or rusty leaves. Put the leaves in a salad spinner and spin the leaves. Fluff up and spin again; the leaves should be quite dry. If a salad spinner isn't available, drain the greens in a large colander or dish rack for 15 minutes; then dry them in a pillowcase by swinging it back and forth very briskly, and stopping to fluff the greens from time to time.

Washed and dried greens may be layered with paper towels and then wrapped in a kitchen towel and refrigerated until you are ready to dress them. If storing excess washed greens, place sheets of paper towels between the washed and dried leaves and store in a dry kitchen towel or plastic bag. Salad greens are best prepared just before serving, but they will keep for as long as two or three days when stored this way. Remember, salad dressing cannot adhere to wet greens and is diluted by excess water. Wet greens also wilt quickly. All loose-leafed greens should be torn, not cut with a knife. The exceptions to this are Iceberg lettuce, cabbage, and other hard-stemmed greens, such as chard, which won't brown when cut with a knife.

Dressing the salad: No matter what the dressing, use only enough to coat the salad lightly. A dressing for simple green salads should be kept to the simplest of ingredients: oil, vinegar or lemon juice, and salt and pepper (always freshly milled). Mild flavored lettuces are best dressed with a ratio of four parts oil to one part vinegar. Stronger leaves require a heartier ratio of three parts oil to one part vinegar. And remember, the ingredients for a cold salad should be cold and the plates should be chilled. Warm salads deserve a warm or tepid plate.

HERBS

Herbs, often prized for their ability to enhance the flavor of different foods, oils, vinegars, and sauces, add even more direct culinary pleasure to a salad when they are used fresh in a dressing or just tossed in with the greens. Western civilization gave us the simple herb garden that flanked the kitchen door. Herbs also found their way into the jewel-like courts of Romanesque cloisters, and the dizzying, interwoven displays of "knots" and topiary viewed from the terraces of the great houses of England, châteaux of France, and villas of Italy.

In Western civilization the Romans were probably the first to set out gardens in their city courtyards and in their country villas. They were a practical lot, cultivating plants as food and to season their dishes, to use as dyes, beauty preparations, perfumes, and aphrodisiacs. There were Roman herbal potions to cure everything from boils to broken hearts. Roses, violets, and lilies were cultivated for their scent and were sprinkled on food. The Romans scattered blossoms throughout their banquet halls, just as the medieval peasant woman would scatter herbs over her dirt floors to halt the ubiquitous stench.

Gardens seemed to fall apart completely during the Dark Ages, until religious orders of the twelfth century began to garden for their own small communities. We think of monasteries as being quite removed from society, but in many cases they were a hub— they were apothecaries, dispensers of drugs, and makers of liqueurs and wines for the local folk.

Their gardens and vineyards went far beyond the monastery walls, but the kitchen, physic, and flower gardens, often in what they call "cloisters," were restorative on every level.

The English garden and its French counterpart, the *potager,* evolved during the sixteenth century, when new and exotic plants were introduced to Europe by explorers. These backdoor gardens boasted dandelion, sorrel, various cresses, purslane, Mediterranean rocket, lamb's lettuce, seedling radish, turnip, mustard, all manner of loose-leaf lettuces, and herbs. Such delectables as tomatoes, potatoes, and maize were being introduced from the New World via Spain and Portugal along with other exotica. The eggplant was introduced by the Moors of Spain via the East. All these vegetables were shrouded in myth and folklore. It would take time before they would be greeted with enthusiasm.

Eighteenth-century America tended such fantasy gardens from Williamsburg to Nantucket. With an unshowy simplicity, the early American garden was a potpourri of flowers, vegetables, and herbs. Herbs can be tucked into the borders of any garden, planted just outside the kitchen door, grown between the stones and bricks of paths, planted on sloping berms, and thyme and rosemary will weep over garden walls. They can grow in clay pots, wooden tubs, or in virtually anything that drains well and retains moisture. They fare well by a sunny kitchen window, whether in the country or in the city. In short, they thrive with little tending, and, what's better, they do not attract bugs—if anything, they drive insects away (except, perhaps, in the case of chives).

Herbs require five to six hours of sun a day. They should be picked in the early morning hours or late in the day, as the heat of the sun drains their oils and potency. (They may be harvested at anytime on a cloudy day.) When harvesting for drying or for making herb oils and vinegars, pick the herbs as soon as the dew dries off their leaves, before the sun begins to dissipate their flavor. As herb plants grow and flower, the energy they use for growth draws potency from their leaves. Pinch the blossoms and use these delicate little flowers to embellish a salad.

To dry herbs, gather them up in small bunches, tie at the base with string, and hang upside down in a dry, well-ventilated basement or attic. If you hang them to dry in your kitchen, keep them away from the stove and sink, to avoid steam and moisture. Remember that dried herbs are stronger than fresh ones. A rule of thumb: When measuring herbs for a recipe, figure that 1 tablespoon of fresh herb is the equivalent of 1 teaspoon of dried. Herbs can be frozen, too. Chop them when fresh and freeze them in sealed plastic containers. Mint on the branch and bunches of chives, wrapped in aluminum foil, can be frozen and then handily snipped with scissors as needed. To keep sage and basil, layer the leaves in coarse salt and store in airtight containers in the refrigerator, where they will keep their freshness throughout the winter months.

Parsley is rich in vitamin A, and as both the curly and Italian types are always available, there is little reason to preserve it.

Of *thyme* there are many varieties, the lemon thyme being my preference in salads or for cooking fish, because of its delicate hint of lemon flavor. The pale blue blossoms can be scattered in many salads or used with poached fresh fruit.

Rosemary, which grows in profusion in California, fares best in the East in pots, brought indoors for the winter. Rosemary is good with meats, roasts, grilled vegetables, and marinades.

Sage works well with meats, roasts, and fatty fish. Different varieties include common garden, red sage, pineapple, and variegated.

French tarragon should be grown from cuttings and rooted, as it doesn't flower or seed, and its flavor lessens after only one season. It is excellent with fish, chicken, or in a simple herb vinaigrette. Russian tarragon is nearly tasteless and often appears in green markets during the winter. Rub a tarragon leaf between your fingers to ensure that it has a light, licorice aroma.

Varieties of *mint* include common garden, spearmint, pineapple, and apple, to mention just a few. My preference is for the straightforward common garden variety for meats (especially lamb), raw fish, and Middle Eastern dishes. The other varieties are marvelous for fruit desserts and sorbets.

Basil is an herb that should be pinched frequently as it grows, to increase the yield. It requires more moisture than most herbs. A natural partner to summer potatoes and pasta salads, it is the star of pesto. In fall, puree the last of the basil crop with olive oil. Store the puree with a film of olive oil on top in small, airtight plastic containers. Don't add the cheese or nuts until you plan to use the pesto. In winter, this muddy emerald puree will give a gush of summer flavor to both hot and cold sauces.

Dill: This feathery leaf and its lacy flower that matures into seeds are natural accompaniments to cucumber, shrimp, and crab salads.

The delicate onion flavor of *chive* is a versatile substitute for its stronger cousins, the scallion and the onion, making chives a natural addition to vinaigrette dressings. The pinkish-purple blossoms resemble bachelor buttons; charged with onion flavor, they can be pulled apart to flavor and decorate salads.

Cilantro is the principal flavor we associate with dishes from the Orient, Mexico, and Brazil. The lower leaves resemble Italian parsley, and the upper leaves are delicate, lacy, and less potent. Most cooks are of either of two schools when it comes to cilantro—some want only a hint of the flavor, and some want a real punch. The upper leaves, with their bluish-white flowers, are sweet and light, found preferable by cooks who don't relish the power of the larger leaves. Cilantro is excellent with fish and shellfish salads, and is a natural accompaniment to the avocado.

Fresh *oregano* is subtle and doesn't at all recall the pungent aroma that rolls out onto the street from most pizza joints. It is superb with grilled meats, and infuses the softer, more delicate goat cheeses with its pleasant flavor when they marinate together in oil.

Pot *marigolds* or *calendula* petals are tossed with salads for their rich, golden color more than for their taste. The petals, dried and crumbled, have long been a poor man's substitute for saffron.

Fennel is a marvel. The flowers and leaves taste strongly of anise or licorice. The bulb of Italian fennel makes wonderful eating, used as an ingredient in winter salads, and the feathery leaves give off an herby, aromatic anise flavor particularly suited to fish dishes. Even dried sticks of fennel can be put to good use when grilling fish: Ignite a handful of dried fennel and throw it over the charcoals at the last minute. The fish will take on an extraordinary savor.

Finally, *nasturtiums* (which seem almost too fanciful to contemplate as food): Both the peppery leaves and delicate blossoms make colorful additions to the greens of a summer salad.

The Greeks were blessed with the olive tree, and from its fruit that noble race produced an oil that offered nourishment, cleansed their skin, soothed their wounds, and lit their nights. The olive flourished throughout the Mediterranean, and both the Greeks and the Romans took it farther afield, where it thrived in France, Spain, Portugal, and northern Africa. Conquistadors brought it to Peru, and California's padres were cultivating olive orchards by the early 1700s. Even so, much of the world's best olive oil comes from Mediterranean olives, and the perfection of that crop is unlikely to change. Producers there dote on the olive oils as winemakers do over their wines. There are indeed other oils, but none as rich or brillant as olive oil.

The process of making olive oil has changed little over the course of the last few thousand years. Traditionally, the oil was extracted by a hand press, and the water and sediment from the flesh of the olives settled out in large holding tanks. The oil itself was stored in urns. The only difference in the procedure today is that the water is separated from the oil by centrifuge. Oils vary from year to year, like wine, and their quality is affected by production techniques and by the type of olives used. Not surprisingly, the best olive oils come from small production farms, many in Tuscany, Provence, and northern Spain.

Olive oils fall into five categories: extra-virgin, superfine virgin, fine virgin, virgin, and pure. These categories are technically determined by the acidity of the oil. Extra-virgin oil is produced from the first

cold pressing of the olives. Each subsequent pressing produces a lesser grade of oil, as hot water and chemicals are added to encourage the full extraction of oil from the fruit. The quality and acidity of extra-virgin olive oil is controlled by the International Olive Oil Council, which guarantees that the oil is untainted by chemical treatment. The acidity of extra-virgin olive oil is 1 percent, in superfine from 1.01 to 1.5 percent, and escalates to 4 percent in virgin. Pure olive oil is yet a lesser grade, often with some amount of virgin oil added for flavor. France, Italy, and Spain have labeling laws to regulate these categories, but those restrictions do not necessarily guarantee the buyer that what he or she is purchasing is a first cold pressing. (It's curious to note that some refined oils, safflower, corn, and peanut, for example, can be bottled with the addition of some first-pressing olive oil, thus allowing the manufacturer to label the bottle of oil "extra-virgin.") So beware.

The best choices of olive oils for salads are those with labels marked "first-pressing virgin," "cold-pressing virgin," or "*extra-vièrge.*" (Using your best oil for frying is pointless, as heat changes the character of olive oil; a lesser-grade oil will do nicely for cooking purposes. Save the good oil to splash on grilled meats, vegetables, and fish, after they have been cooked.) When oil is made from ripe olives (which are black), the flavor will be sweet and the color golden; this is usually the preference of French manufacturers. The Italians prefer pressing a less ripe green olive which results in a greener cast to the color and a sharper taste. Both are wonderful. Use only the less expensive third- and fourth-pressings when making your own herbs, garlic- or hot pepper-flavored oils. Olive oil should be stored in glazed clay, glass, stainless-steel, or tin containers, and never in plastic, copper, and iron, as these materials will alter the taste of the oil. It should be kept in a cool, dry place, never in the sun, and never in the refrigerator. Olive oil admirably contains no cholesterol and weighs in at 125 calories a tablespoon.

After olive oil, the oils used most often in this book are nut oils. They are not as versatile as olive oil, but, if more limited in their use, they can be every bit as brilliant. They are fragrant, sensuous, and strong in the flavor of the nut from which they are made. Walnut, hazelnut, and almond oils are quite potent, so use them with discretion or mix the oil with a blander oil, such as vegetable or soy. (Peanut oil is highly refined and reflects little true peanut taste; it is used mostly for frying and sautéing.) When making a salad that includes walnuts, hazelnuts, almonds, or grapeseeds, use the "matching" oil in your dressing.

Walnut oil is best when used on hearty fall and winter lettuces, such as chicory, endive, and *frisée* (blanched chicory). It tastes especially good with game—pheasant, quail, partridge, turkey—as well as with sharp and pungent blue cheeses.

Hazelnut oil goes well with broiled or grilled fish and sturdy greens, such as chard, spinach, and mustard and turnip greens.

Almond oil is especially strong in taste and aroma, and goes beautifully with sautéed sole or flounder, or with any dish you might *amandine* (trout, for example). A small amount added to the cooking butter will infuse the fish with a suggestion of almond flavor.

Peanut oil has been so refined in this country that virtually all the peanut flavor has been removed. Chinese peanut oils are rich in peanut flavor, though. From France there are lightly-flavored peanut oils, and one or two good brands are produced in the United States. The most flavorful and the best can be found at health food stores and fancy food shops.

Sesame oil is pressed from sesame seeds. Oriental sesame oils are orange in color and intense in sesame flavor because they are made from toasted sesame seeds. Most of these are produced in Japan, China, or Taiwan, and these are the oils you will use for recipes in this book. Other sesame oils are pale yellow in color, absolutely bland in flavor, and usually sold at health-food stores. They will not enhance a salad. Because sesame oils vary so widely, taste an unfamiliar brand before using it in a recipe, and use it sparingly. Small amounts of the Oriental types are delicious when used in squid and lobster salads, with steamed or fried fish, and as a light seasoning for green bean, artichoke, and Oriental chicken salads.

Hot oils are made from chile peppers and are used to flavor sesame, peanut, and vegetable oils. Most come from the Orient, and they run the gamut from a polite peppery flavor to one that can blow your head off. The Brazilians offer chile oils of dynamite potency. They pack a jar with minuscule chiles and cover the mass with palm oil or a bland cooking oil.

This "packing" oil may be used in driblets, but it is the chile itself that the Brazilians eat with their grilled fish, meats, and *feijoadas.*

To make your own hot pepper oils, wash and thoroughly sun-dry whole small chiles or hot peppers. Pack a sterilized glass jar or bottle with the peppers and cover them with corn, peanut, vegetable, or light olive oil; cover tightly. Allow to sit in a cool, light (but not sunny) place for a month or so. The peppery intensity of the oil will increase as long as the chiles remain in the oil. The oil, an excellent preservative for the peppers, may be used for all dishes requiring "hot" oil.

Spiced oils, flavored with ginger, lemon oil, and beefsteak leaves, come to us from Japan. The beefsteak leaves give off a slightly smoky taste, and the others reflect their own individual flavors. These oils are used mostly in Oriental cooking but can add a subtle Oriental accent when used in marinating or grilling food.

Herbed oils are very pleasing to our Western palates and are the most adaptable of all the flavored oils available. Use them for dressing salads, making marinades, and for grilling, sautéing, and basting meat, fish, or vegetables. Herbed oils are quite often beautifully packaged and attractive to the buyer, but they easily can be made at home. The strength and quality of the finished oil depends on the pungency of the herbs you use in making them.

To make herbed oil, wash and dry any combination of herbs (say thyme, rosemary, and oregano). The

herb leaves maybe left on the stems or pulled off. For a stronger flavor, bruise the leaves slightly. For every cup of herbs, use 1½ to 2 cups of olive oil (second or third pressing). Place the herbs in a crock, bottle, or jar, cover with the oil, and seal tightly. Store in a cool, dark place for a week to 10 days. Check the flavor for intensity, and, when it is to your liking, strain the oil into a clean bottle, pressing lightly on the herbs to extract the oil. You may add a few fresh sprigs of herbs and a peeled garlic clove if you wish. Store in a cool, dark place.

Remember: Never buy oil if you have reason to think it has been stored in the sun. If you do not customarily use large quantities of olive oil or nut oils, buy them in small quantities. Oils spoil easily, especially in warm weather, and become rancid. Nut oils should be stored in the refrigerator. Do not refrigerate olive oil, but do store it in a cool, dark place. To test the quality of olive oil, place a few tablespoons in a bowl and refrigerate it. If small crystals appear on the surface, the oil is most likely cold pressed extra-virgin. If it becomes buttery, it is an oil of lesser quality (or perhaps a combination of olive oil and another oil).

Good oil is like a condiment, meant to be splashed on grilled meats, fish, and vegetables, and used in salad dressings. Unlike vegetable and frying oils which can be heated to 365 degrees, good olive and nut oils begin to burn at 280 degrees. Cook with a lesser-grade olive oil when preparing dishes that call for it, as it is pointless to use your best.

What makes a salad good is the quality of its basic ingredients: the greens and their dressing, which is usually oil and vinegar. Vinegar is cheap, compared to some of the other ingredients we use to dress a salad, but good vinegar deserves its price, and we have become accustomed to the flavor of good vinegars as our tastes have become more sophisticated. As good wine is aged, so goes the process of making good vinegar. *Vinaigre*, which we translate from the French as "vinegar," means "soured wine." Naturally fermented beverages, such as wine, apple cider, and malt, will eventually sour and turn to vinegar when aerated. When any of these liquids are left to stand over a period of time, a veil of bacteria called a "mother" will form. This starts out as a small disk of film and grows to a gelatinous mass resembling a jellyfish. The mother keeps the vinegar alive, producing more and more bacteria in the parent liquid, turning it to vinegar.

The making of good vinegar is a craft that goes at least as far back as the fourteenth century, when a guild was formed to protect the vinegar makers in the French city of Orléans. *Vinaigre à l'Ancienne*, meaning "made by the Orléans process," may still appear on bottles of properly aged French vinegars. The traditional method still used today by producers of good vinegar is to store the wine in wooden casks kept in cool, dark cellars or caves. Usually the casks are old wine barrels, with spigots at the bottom from which the producer can "taste test" his product.

Once it reaches the desired tartness and flavor, the vinegar is siphoned off and then bottled, and more wine or cider is added to the keg, beginning the process all over again.

Vinegar-making kits are available, and mothers can be ordered by mail to start home production of made-from-scratch vinegar. But you can start your own vinegar without a kit. Just leave a crock or Mason jar, one-quarter to one-half full of white wine, red wine, or cider, loosely covered, in a cool, dark place. In a few months, and with a little luck, you will have a mother that will turn out vinegar for life.

Making good vinegar depends on starting with the best ingredients: good wine or cider. When I make wine vinegar, my only rule is to keep adding as similar a wine as possible to what is already bubbling in each crock, white or red. No doubt I've thrown a few Champagne bubbles into the white, but I keep the Chianti separate from the Burgundy. Once you have your supply going, start putting up your vinegars in clean wine bottles and cork them tightly. It is that simple.

The varieties of vinegars are endless. Every region of France that produces grapes for wine, from Champagne to Provence, produces vinegar, as do the wine-producing regions of Italy and California. Sherry from Spain is made into vinegar, and so are rice wines from China and Japan.

Sherry vinegar is rich and full bodied, with a slightly sweet aftertaste. It complements fruit, cheese, and duck salads.

Rice wine vinegars work well with delicate fish salads and with cooked vegetable salads.

Aceto balsamico is Italy's—if not the world's—best vinegar. Of all commercially made vinegars, I think balsamic is the most delicious. It is made from sweet wine, high in acid and very aromatic, and is bottled at different agings. You can find balsamic vinegar that is 80 years old. The older it is, the more mellow and complex the taste, and the more expensive the pleasure. The prices can, in fact, get pretty heady, but some of the older vinegars are so delicious that they can be sipped from a spoon or sprinkled drop by drop on fruit. (Serious dieters can splash it on most salads and forgo the oil entirely.) A dressing prepared with balsamic vinegar requires no additional condiments—no mustard, not even salt—just mix it with a little Italian virgin olive oil and a little freshly milled pepper.

Apple cider vinegars lack the bite of wine-based vinegars. My experience has been that the higher-priced ones are fruitier, more robust, and explosive. They work well with warm potato salads, cabbage salads and slaws, and with wilted salads that include bacon drippings in place of oil.

It is at the end of summer when the garden and markets are overrun with green herbs, and at those times during the berry season when you are freezing the quantities of fruit you can't possibly eat fresh, that you make your fragrant herb and fruit vinegars. Distilled white and white wine vinegars are best for making both herb and fruit vinegars. These light vinegars take on the colors of the herbs and fruits, and the delicate taste of the whites takes on their flavors nicely (as opposed to the red vinegar varieties, which tend to absorb the flavors. White wine vinegar will be a more acidic base for flavored vinegars than white distilled vinegar.

To make herb vinegar, wash and dry the herbs on their stems using about 3 tablespoons of herb leaves for each quart of vinegar. Bruise the herbs slightly and place them in a clean, clear glass bottle or Mason jar. Pour the vinegar over the herbs, replace the cork or cap, and set the bottle in a sunny window for two weeks. Store in a cool spot for another two weeks. Taste for strength, and filter the vinegar into sterilized clear bottles. Add a sprig of the identifying herb, cork tightly, and store. Use only one type of herb, not a combination, for the most successful flavorings. Herbed vinegars are wonderful in salads, sauces, stews, marinades, and grilled and sautéed dishes. Mint vinegar is excellent with lamb and fruit salads. (Country folk add a teaspoon or two of mint vinegar to sugar and mix it with ice water or sparkling water for a summer cooler.)

Thyme and lemon thyme vinegars are delicious to dress fish salads, basil vinegar for tomatoes, crab, and lobster, and sage vinegar for meats and fowl. Garlic, garlic chives, chive, and chive buds make a spirited vinegar for meat and vegetable salads. Nasturtium leaves give vinegar a light peppery taste and are a pretty conceit. Tarragon vinegar is sweet, perfumy, and almost everyone's favorite. It is, of course, excellent with chicken and vegetable salads.

To make fruit vinegar, place 2 cups of strawberries, raspberries, blueberries, or blackberries (washed and drained) in a sterilized bottle or jar. Pour in 1 quart of distilled white or white wine vinegar. Cover and let stand in a sunny window for two or three days. Taste for fruitiness, and, when the vinegar is to your liking, strain it into an enameled or stainless-steel pan. Add ½ to ¾ cup sugar, bring to a boil, and simmer for 10 minutes. Skim, if necessary, and cool. Store in tightly sealed sterile jars or wine bottles. A little bit of unsweetened fruit extract (available in fancy food shops) may be added just before bottling for a richer and fruitier flavor.

Fruit vinegars complement warm chicken, pork, and game salads, as well as *salades composées* and salads that include fruits. They are especially good for making a warm sauce and can be used in place of wine.

Remember: Vinegars are acidic and, therefore, corrosive, and should be stored in glass or glazed ceramic containers. Likewise, when cooking, marinating, or making dressings with vinegar, use glass, enameled, or stainless-steel cookware. Do *not* use copper, zinc, aluminum, or cast iron. The acid level of vinegar is related to the quality of the vinegar; good quality vinegar can be as high as 7 percent acidity, and cheaper varieties as low as 4 percent.

Very acidic wine vinegars (homemade wine vinegars can be especially acidic) may be diluted with a little red or white wine. Always taste a vinegar before making a dressing; this way you will understand its effect and strength. The heartier red wine vinegars are best for meat and wild fowl salads, and the more delicate tasting white wine vinegars are a perfect foil for fish salads and tender lettuces. Lemon, lime, or orange juice is often substituted for the acidic flavor of vinegar in dressings and in marinades, and the addition of the zest of these citric fruits gives an extra spark to dressings as well.

WINES

There is never a single answer to the question of which wine should accompany which food. This is particularly true for salads. Indeed, vinegar and wine are classic enemies, and many will tell you they do not mix at all. Relaxed eating, however, is a time that blurs the line between enemies and friends. The wines suggested in this book will agree with non-vinegar dressings and survive the vinegar dressings, even if they are not perfectly harmonious with this traditional foe. Where there is a vinegar-based dressing, be assured the wine will take to its other ingredients, and once one has had a few glasses and is enjoying life and the rest of the salad, the conflict of vinegar and wine will be forgotten in the enjoyment of the day. Psychology is often more important than chemistry. The wine suggestions for each of these salads are thus only that—one indication of a possible match.

Wines for these salads fit into several categories. First, there are the fairly simple dry and semidry white wines, which suit uncomplicated summer salad recipes—those made from plain vegetables and plain seafood. These wines include American Sauvignon Blancs and Chenin Blancs (from the Northwest and California), Italian whites, such as Pinot Grigios and Orvietos, and certain French white wines, such as a Sancerre or a Mâcon Villages. A rosé from Provence, the Rhône, or California can be a pleasant alternative. In winter, light reds are added, though they can be used in summer as well.

A second category of wines applies to salads in which certain cheeses and richer foods, such as lobster, predominate. Here, a fuller-bodied white wine

is appropriate. It can also be an opportunity for treating guests, and yourself, to one of the better whites that you can afford. Good choices might include a white Hermitage from the Rhône, a richer white Burgundy—such as a Meursault or Puligny Montrachet from one of the finer growers—or a full-bodied American Chardonnay.

The third wine category is one for spicy salads that include ingredients such as chilies, curries, or salsas. It is difficult to find wines that will hold up to these dishes at all, and a cold beer can be an attractive alternative. There are, nonetheless, a few good wine possibilities: A sturdy rosé (such as those produced by Tempier in Provence) and, alternatively and perhaps better, a dry white Muscat from Oregon or Alsace, or a Kabinett Riesling.

The fourth category includes hearty salads made with various meats, herbs, and strong-tasting vegetables such as fennel, cabbage, and fresh horseradish. Generally, a wine from the Beaujolais family—ranging from the nouveau and the softer, fruitier Fleuries and Julienas, to the much sturdier Moulin-à-Vents—is a happy match.

Throughout the series of wine selections, there are often indications as to growers or owners. The key word is "indication." Some of the wines will be available to you and some will not. What is important is to buy what you can afford. The better growers will tend, on balance, to produce better-tasting wines. The ones listed here meet my criteria, and if you can get them at prices that meet your pocketbook, I think that you will enjoy them.   —Yves-Andres Istel

The freshest greens combined with salt and pepper, dressed with a little oil and vinegar, make the classic palate cleanser. Cruets of oil and vinegar for mix-your-own dressing are still the norm in many homes and restaurants. Though most people's preference is to use leafy, soft greens, you should use whatever lettuces you like best. I believe that a green salad with the proper combination of oil and vinegar is as personal as one's morning coffee.

Here are some vinaigrette recipes as guides, and a mayonnaise recipe, for what would some salads be without it?

VINAIGRETTE

Ingredients

¼ cup good-quality red wine vinegar

1 teaspoon dry mustard

1½ teaspoons Dijon mustard

Salt and freshly milled black pepper, to taste

¾ cup olive oil (or a bit more, depending on the acidity of the vinegar)

Method

Manual method: In a bowl, whisk together the vinegar and the seasonings; mix thoroughly, until the salt dissolves. Begin adding the oil, drop by drop, whisking until emulsified. Then begin adding the oil in a thin stream and whisk constantly until creamy and smooth.

Machine method: Using a food processor or blender, combine the vinegar with the seasonings and process until the salt dissolves.

With the machine running, slowly add the oil, drop by drop, processing until emulsified. Gradually begin

adding the oil in a thin steady stream, and process until it is well incorporated and the vinaigrette is creamy.

Store in the refrigerator. This vinaigrette will keep indefinitely.

Makes 1 cup

HERB VINAIGRETTE

To the above vinaigrette, add 1 teaspoon each of chopped chives, parsley, and tarragon. This vinaigrette should be used immediately.

CREAMY VINAIGRETTE

Ingredients

1 large egg, separated

1½ teaspoons Dijon mustard

Salt and freshly milled pepper, to taste

¼ cup light tarragon wine vinegar

¾ cup vegetable oil or peanut oil

¼ cup olive oil

2 tablespoons *crème fraîche* or heavy cream

Method

Using a wire whisk or a food processor, combine the egg yolk and half of the egg white with the mustard and salt and pepper. Beat until smooth.

Gradually add the vinegar and then the oils, in a thin steady stream and beat until creamy and smooth.

Add the *crème fraîche* and beat until thoroughly combined.

Refrigerate in a covered container for up to 1 week. Let come to room temperature before using.

Makes about 1¼ cups

MAYONNAISE

Ingredients

4 egg yolks, at room temperature

1 teaspoon Dijon mustard

Salt and freshly milled white pepper, to taste

Dash of cayenne pepper

1½ cups olive oil, or ¾ cup olive oil and ¾ cup vegetable oil

2 tablespoons fresh lemon juice

1 tablespoon boiling water

Method

Place the egg yolks, mustard, salt, pepper, and cayenne in a blender or food processor and beat at high speed for 2 minutes, or until creamy.

With the motor running, gradually add all of the oil, in a slow, thin stream. Process until smooth.

Add the lemon juice and taste for seasoning; blend until smooth.

Add the boiling water and mix for 2 to 3 seconds, just until incorporated.

Refrigerate the mayonnaise for up to 5 days in a covered container.

Makes about 2 cups

LIME MAYONNAISE

Ingredients

2 egg yolks, at room temperature

Juice and grated zest of 1 large lime

1 cup extra-virgin olive oil

1 tablespoon boiling water

2 tablespoons heavy cream

Salt and freshly milled white pepper

Method

In a blender or food processor, beat the egg yolks until thick.

Add the lime juice and zest and process until creamy.

With the machine running, add the oil in a thin steady stream and blend until emulsified.

Add the boiling water. Add the cream and process until very smooth.

Season with salt and pepper to taste.

Makes 1½ cups

SUMMER SALAD

My favorite salad for a boiling-hot summer day is a combination of crunchy, crisp, ice-cold vegetables, chopped and chilled, and served with a little bread and sweet butter and a glass of cold white wine. If you're too lazy to pull a cork, soda water with a slice of lemon is easier. A spare, but enjoyable, feast.

Ingredients

1 bunch red radishes, trimmed and thinly sliced into rounds

1 bunch scallions, trimmed and thinly sliced into rounds (including 2 inches of the green)

1 medium cucumber, peeled, seeded, and finely diced

½ small bunch fresh dill, chopped

2 cups plain yogurt

Salt and freshly milled white pepper

Fresh dill sprigs

Method

In a glass or ceramic bowl, fold the vegetables and dill into the yogurt and season with salt and pepper to taste.

Cover and refrigerate for at least 1 hour, or until well chilled.

Sprinkle with the dill sprigs and serve cold.

Serves 2 to 4

Calories: 2 servings—160 per person
4 servings—80 per person

Wine: Sauvignon Blanc

BLACK BEANS, ASPARAGUS, AND GOAT CHEESE

Spring, of course, is the best time for asparagus and our earliest cravings are sated by simply poaching and serving. But as the season ends, I like to spark it up with bitter greens and smooth it out with black beans and fresh mild goat cheese.

Ingredients

3 cups chicken stock or broth

4 ounces dried black beans

1 jalapeño pepper, split lengthwise

2 tablespoons olive oil

2 yellow bell peppers, seeded, deveined, and cut into long thin julienne

2 chocolate or green bell peppers, seeded, deveined, and cut into long thin julienne

2 bunches watercress, washed and dried

1 bunch dandelion greens, washed and dried

20 thin asparagus spears, trimmed and steamed until crisp-tender

8 ounces soft fresh goat cheese, at room temperature

Dressing

¼ cup hot red pepper oil

¼ cup extra-virgin olive oil

¼ cup cider vinegar

¼ teaspoon ground coriander

Salt

Cayenne pepper

Method

Bring the stock, black beans, and jalapeño to a boil in a medium saucepan over high heat. Reduce the heat to low and simmer for 1 hour, or until the beans are just tender but not mushy. (Add water, if necessary, to keep the beans covered with liquid.) Drain and set aside.

Warm the oil in a large skillet over moderate heat. Add the yellow peppers and cook, tossing, until wilted. Remove with tongs to a plate.

Add the chocolate peppers and cook, tossing, until wilted. Remove with tongs; add to the yellow peppers.

Trim the greens and mound on 4 dinner plates.

Scatter the peppers and asparagus over the greens and sprinkle with the beans.

Drop little spoonfuls of the goat cheese over the top.

In a bowl, whisk together the dressing ingredients and season with salt and cayenne to taste.

Serve at room temperature and pass the dressing separately.

Serves 4

Calories: salad—338 per serving
dressing—80 calories per tablespoon

Wine: Zinfandel (Alexander Valley Vineyard)

GRILLED VEGETABLE SALAD

When grilled, vegetables take on such a unique flavor, it's as though they become a completely new food. Eggplant is particularly good as the flesh becomes very tender and moist. Choose ones with a smooth taut skin that gives a little but bounces back when pressed with your thumb. Summer offers them in a variety of sizes and colors; save the bulbous, ebony balloons for stuffing, pickling, frying, or ratatouille.

Ingredients

12 ripe red plum tomatoes

8 baby yellow squash

8 baby zucchini

4 Oriental or Italian baby purple eggplants

4 baby white eggplants

About ½ cup olive oil

Coarse (kosher) salt and freshly milled black pepper

Vegetable oil, to brush the grill

¼ cup balsamic vinegar

Method

Prepare the fire and set a large rack over the grill.

Keeping the vegetables intact at the stem ends, cut all of the vegetables except the tomatoes lengthwise into ¼-inch slices. (Sprinkle the eggplants with salt and set aside to "sweat" for 15 to 20 minutes. Dry well with paper towels, squeezing out the excess moisture.) Brush the vegetables with the olive oil and sprinkle with salt and pepper.

When the coals are ash-covered and glowing, brush the grill with vegetable oil and arrange the vegetables on the hot grill.

As the vegetables soften, fan out the slices and cook until browned and wilted on one side. Turn over with tongs and cook for about 5 minutes more.

Remove to a serving platter and splash with the vinegar and additional olive oil, if you wish. Serve hot.

Serves 4

Calories: 235 per serving

Wine: Ch. Ste. Michelle Pinot Noir

PARSLEY AND BULGUR SALAD

Bulgur wheat and, of course, mint are widely used in Middle Eastern cooking. This is a salad with textures and flavors that shine through when individually chopped. It is best served with whole wheat pita.

Ingredients

¼ cup bulgur wheat (cracked wheat)

3 cups chopped fresh parsley

10 yellow cherry tomatoes

1 small red onion, finely diced

¼ cup chopped fresh mint leaves

Juice and grated zest of 1 lemon

2½ cups extra-virgin olive oil

Salt

Method

Place the bulgur in a bowl and add boiling water to cover by about 1 inch. Set aside for 1½ hours.

Toss together the parsley, tomatoes, onion, and mint in a large bowl.

Drain the bulgur and squeeze well with your hands to remove any excess water. Turn the wheat onto a towel and fluff to separate the grains. Add to the other ingredients.

Add the lemon juice and zest and toss. Drizzle the oil over the salad and season with salt to taste. Cover and chill well before serving.

Serves 2

Calories: 393 calories per serving

Wine: Bourgogne les Clous (À de Villaine)

MEDITERRANEAN SALAD

This salad is almost a *Niçoise,* and indeed, if you wish, you can make it one by adding potatoes and tuna fish. Anchovies may be served on the side if you are not sure of your guest's tastes. I like to enhance the flavor by serving anchovy butter with the bread.

Ingredients

½ cup rosemary-flavored olive oil (see page 27)

1 white bell pepper, seeded, deveined, and cut into medium julienne

Coarse (kosher) salt

2 mild red chile peppers, seeded, deveined, and cut into thin julienne

1 green frying pepper, seeded, deveined, and cut into long fine julienne

1 yellow bell pepper, seeded, deveined, and cut into medium julienne

4 garlic cloves, slivered

2 large ripe tomatoes, peeled, seeded, and coarsely chopped

Freshly milled black pepper

6 green oil-cured olives

8 large basil leaves, cut into julienne

4 hard-cooked eggs, peeled

8 flat anchovy fillets

Method

Warm the oil in a large skillet over moderate heat. Add the white pepper and sauté until wilted. Season with salt and remove with tongs to a plate. Sauté the remaining peppers, one type at a time, as you did the white pepper, season, and add to the plate, keeping each type separate from the others.

Sauté the garlic in the remaining oil until golden; remove with a slotted spoon and set aside.

Add the tomatoes and sauté until warmed through. Season with salt and pepper and divide between 2 dinner plates, mounding on one side of the plate.

Arrange each type of pepper in a separate mound.

Place 3 olives on the side of each plate. Sprinkle basil over the tomatoes. Place 2 eggs on each plate. Crisscross 2 anchovies over the top of each egg. Sprinkle the garlic over the salad.

Season with additional pepper and serve.

Serves 2

Calories: 500 per serving

Wine: Tavel or Bandol rosé (Domaine Tempier)

PENNE AND FRESH TOMATO SAUCE

This pasta served with icebox-cold tomato sauce cools off on the way from the kitchen to the table.

Ingredients

Fresh tomato sauce

4 large ripe red tomatoes, cored and quartered

Large bunch fresh basil

4 garlic cloves, crushed

¾ cup extra-virgin olive oil

¼ cup balsamic vinegar

Salt and freshly milled black pepper, to taste

Pasta

1 pound penne

1 tablespoon extra-virgin olive oil

Method

In a food processor, combine all of the sauce ingredients and process, pulsing on and off, until very roughly chopped.

Pour into a bowl, cover, and refrigerate until well chilled.

Cook the pasta in salted boiling water until tender. Drain well.

While the pasta is still hot, toss with the oil. Turn into a serving dish.

Spoon the chilled tomato sauce over the pasta and serve.

Serves 4

Calories: 818 per serving

Wine: Pinot Grigio

SPAGHETTI SQUASH SALAD

We think of spaghetti squash as a winter vegetable, but it makes its debut at the farm stands in early August. Treat it like its namesake, spaghetti. When served up with spicy chiles and an Oriental dressing, it is elevated from the "ho-hum, squash again" syndrome.

Ingredients

1 medium spaghetti squash

3 tablespoons olive oil

3 yellow bell peppers, seeded, deveined, and cut into medium julienne

1 green frying pepper, seeded, deveined, and cut into fine julienne

2 jalapeño peppers, seeded, deveined, and cut into fine julienne

1 hot red chile pepper, seeded, deveined, and cut into fine julienne

1 mild green chile pepper, seeded, deveined, and cut into medium julienne

⅓ cup sesame seeds

Salt

Dressing

½ cup Oriental sesame oil

2 tablespoons extra-virgin olive oil

¼ cup ginger vinegar (see page 30)

1 teaspoon wasabi or Coleman's dry mustard

Salt

Method

In a large pot of water, set over high heat, boil the spaghetti squash whole for 1 hour, or until the flesh can be pierced easily with a kitchen fork.

When the squash is almost cooked, warm the oil in a large skillet over moderate heat.

Add the yellow peppers and sauté until wilted. Remove with tongs to a plate.

Sauté the remaining peppers, one type at a time, as you did the yellow peppers.

Add the sesame seeds to the skillet and toast, stirring, until just slightly colored. Remove at once and drain on paper towels.

In a bowl, whisk together the dressing ingredients and season with salt to taste.

When the squash is cooked, place it on its side, and cut out an oval "top." Carefully set the top aside. Scoop out the seeds; discard.

With a fork, gently pull strands of squash away from the sides of the shell and set them in a bowl. Toss gently to separate and fluff the strands.

Add all of the peppers, dressing, and sesame seeds. Toss gently to mix.

Return the salad to the shell and serve at room temperature.

Serves 4

Calories: 500 per serving

Wine: Eschol white (Trefethen) or chilled Soave

TOMATOES AND FRESH MOZZARELLA

Mozzarella is best when it is bought the day it is made. Stored in water in the refrigerator, it retains its freshness and moistness. The water buffalo milk variety is the true Italian version available at some Italian and fine food markets. The bush basil is a miniature version of the hearty basil plant and is eaten stem and all. The tomatoes must be bursting ripe. This is a simple but luxurious treatment, a perfect lunch dish or introduction to a summer supper.

Ingredients

4 large ripe red tomatoes, cut into ¼-inch slices

12 ounces fresh buffalo or whole milk mozzarella cheese, cut into ¼-inch slices

¼ cup extra-virgin olive oil

Coarse (kosher) salt and freshly milled black pepper

1 sprig bush basil, or 8 large basil leaves

Method

Alternate the tomato and cheese slices on a serving platter.

Drizzle with the olive oil and sprinkle with the salt and pepper to taste.

Place the basil on top and serve at room temperature.

Serves 4

Calories: 426 calories per serving

Wine: Pinot Grigio

ARUGULA AND HERBED CHEESE WITH FRIED GARLIC

This pleasant little luncheon salad is easy to make and could be a particularly nice accompaniment to grilled butterflied leg of lamb or veal chops. Treat the garlic as you would croutons or bacon.

Ingredients

4-ounce log semisoft goat cheese

1 large sprig fresh oregano, rosemary, or thyme

½ cup extra-virgin olive oil

4 large garlic cloves, cut into paper-thin slivers

12 yellow cherry tomatoes, halved

3 tablespoons balsamic vinegar

Salt and freshly milled black pepper

2 small bunches arugula, washed and dried

Method

Prepare the cheese: At least one day ahead, place the goat cheese in a shallow dish. Bruise the herb leaves by squeezing them between your fingers. Place the sprig on top of the cheese. Coat the cheese with about 1 tablespoon of the oil, pressing the herb into the top of the cheese.

Wrap tightly in plastic wrap, weigh down with a heavy plate (to press the herb into the cheese), and refrigerate.

Prepare the salad: Remove the goat cheese from the refrigerator and let it come to room temperature.

Meanwhile, coat a small skillet with about 1 teaspoon of the oil and set over low heat.

When the oil begins to warm, add the slivered garlic and toast, turning occasionally, until golden. Drain on paper towels.

Scoop out most of the seeds from the tomato halves and fill the well with some of the softened cheese.

In a large bowl, combine the remaining oil with the vinegar and season with salt and pepper to taste. Add the arugula and toss until well coated.

Divide the arugula between 2 plates, add the tomatoes, and sprinkle the garlic over each plate. Serve.

Serves 2

Calories: salad—355 per serving
dressing—75 per tablespoon

Wine: Chianti (Ruffino)

Mustard greens, beet tops, and Swiss chard are neglected greens that are once again gaining favor in our kitchens, and they make a nice change from more commonly used salad greens. Try to buy small chard so that you can use the ribs. This hearty, strong leaf responds well to the strong blue cheese and the pungent nuts and oil.

Ingredients

1 bunch small ruby Swiss chard leaves, washed and cut into thin ribbons (including the thin ribs)

1 bunch small white Swiss chard, washed and cut into thin ribbons (including the thin ribs)

¼ cup hazelnut oil

¼ cup safflower oil

4 garlic cloves, crushed

¼ cup slivered hazelnuts

¼ cup raspberry vinegar (see page 31)

Salt and freshly milled black pepper

4 ounces *Bleu de Bresse* or semisoft blue cheese, at room temperature

Method

Divide the chard leaves onto two separate plates.

In a skillet, warm the oils over low heat. Add the garlic and sauté until golden brown. Remove with a slotted spoon and drain on paper towels.

Add the hazelnuts and toast until lightly golden. Remove with a slotted spoon and drain on paper towels.

Add the vinegar to the skillet and season with salt and pepper to taste. Cook, stirring, until heated through; set the dressing aside.

Sprinkle each salad with the garlic and hazelnuts. Drizzle on the warm dressing. Cut the cheese into thin slices and arrange over each serving.

Serves 2

Calories: salad—435 per serving
dressing—62 per tablespoon

Wine: Moulin-à-Vent or other cru Beaujolais

SMOKED FISH WITH BLUE CHEESE, NEW POTATOES, AND RED ONION

This very oily fish is best grilled and sublime when smoked. If smoked bluefish is not available, substitute smoked whitefish.

Ingredients

4 slices smoked bacon

½ cup sour cream, at room temperature

Zest of ½ lemon cut into julienne

¼ cup chopped fresh parsley

1 large bunch leaf lettuce, washed, dried, and torn into bite-size pieces

20 small red new potatoes or culls with a strip of peel removed around the center, boiled in lightly salted water until fork-tender

1 medium red onion, very thinly sliced

8 ounces smoked bluefish or codfish, flaked

2 ounces blue cheese, crumbled and at room temperature

Method

In a large skillet, render the bacon slowly over moderate heat until browned and crispy. Drain on paper towels and set aside.

Remove the skillet from the heat and let the drippings cool slightly. Whisk in the sour cream until smooth.

Spoon the dressing into a bowl and whisk in the lemon zest and parsley.

Divide the lettuce between 2 plates.

Mound the potatoes over the lettuce.

Separate the onion slices into rings. Scatter over the potatoes.

Drizzle the dressing over the potatoes and onion rings.

Crumble the bacon and sprinkle over the dressing. Scatter the flaked bluefish and the blue cheese over all. Serve at room temperature.

Serves 2

Calories: 769 per serving

Wine: Pouilly Fumé or California Fumé Blanc

COBB SALAD

Cobb salad supposedly originated at that old war-horse of a restaurant, The Brown Derby. Rather than mixing it up in a bowl, keep the ingredients separate—it tastes better.

Ingredients

Salad

2 large chicken breast halves, poached, chilled, skinned, and cut into medium dice

¼ pound Roquefort cheese, crumbled and at room temperature

2 small heads romaine, washed and cut into thin ribbons

3 ripe red tomatoes, peeled, seeded, and diced

⅓ pound slab bacon, sliced, cooked, and chopped

Buttermilk Dressing

½ cup sour cream

½ cup homemade mayonnaise (see page 36)

½ cup buttermilk

¼ cup sliced scallions

¼ cup chopped fresh parsley

2 tablespoons white wine vinegar

1¼ teaspoons celery seed

1 teaspoon chopped fresh tarragon leaves

Salt and freshly milled black pepper

Method

Divide the salad ingredients between two plates and arrange in rows, side by side.

In a food processor, combine all of the dressing ingredients and mix until creamy and smooth. Season with salt and pepper to taste.

Serve the salad at room temperature and pass the dressing separately.

Serves 2

Calories: salad—616 per serving
dressing—43 per tablespoon

Wine: Meursault

SALAD OF RAW BEEF WITH SAGE BLOSSOMS

What's raw beef to us is *carpaccio* to the Italians. Protein and vitamins are packed onto this plate, with a little romance sprinkled on in the form of sage blossoms.

Ingredients

Salad

8 ounces lean eye of round or filet of beef

1 bunch ruby Swiss chard, washed and cut into bite-size pieces

8 ounces Romano or Parmesan cheese, in one piece

2 large sage leaves, cut into julienne

8 to 10 sage blossoms

16 black *Niçoise* olives

Dressing

⅓ cup extra-virgin olive oil

3 tablespoons chive vinegar (see page 30)

Salt and freshly milled black pepper

Method

Wrap the beef in waxed paper and freeze for 30 minutes.

Arrange the chard on a serving plate.

Using a home electric slicer or cheese wire, shave the cheese into thin sheets.

Remove the beef from the freezer and cut it into paper-thin slices with a slicer or very sharp knife.

Arrange the beef over the chard and place the cheese on top.

Sprinkle the salad with the sage, sage blossoms, and olives.

Whisk together the dressing ingredients and drizzle over the salad just before serving.

Serves 2

Calories: salad—783 per serving
dressing—70 per tablespoon

Wine: Bandol red (Tempier)

This salad is a rainbow of flavors. When composed with imagination, certain combinations of fruits, meats, and vegetables make sense. Don't go crazy looking for all of the ingredients. Just use what the garden and markets offer you.

Ingredients

4 small boneless skinless chicken breast halves

Salt and freshly milled black pepper

12 Egyptian onions or pearl onions

4 large garlic cloves, unpeeled

8 ounces red runner beans with their flowers or other fresh green beans, trimmed and halved lengthwise

¼ pound unsalted butter

¼ cup plus 2 tablespoons olive oil

2 teaspoons sugar

¼ cup blackberry or raspberry vinegar (see page 31)

⅛ teaspoon ground cloves

2 small heads red-leaf lettuce, washed and separated

1 small red bell pepper, seeded, deveined, and cut into medium julienne

½ mango

12 blackberries with stems

Method

Place the chicken breasts between two sheets of waxed paper and gently pound to flatten slightly. Season lightly with salt and pepper.

In a pot of boiling water, blanch the onions for 2 to 3 minutes. Remove in a slotted spoon and plunge into cold water; remove the skins and set aside.

In the same boiling water, blanch the garlic for 8 to 10 minutes, until soft. Cool, peel, set aside.

In another pot of lightly salted boiling water, cook the beans until tender. Drain and cool under cold water; drain again.

In a large skillet, melt the butter with 2 tablespoons of the oil over moderate heat. Add the onions and garlic and sauté until golden; distribute them around the edge of the pan.

Add the chicken to the skillet and sauté for 4 to 5 minutes on each side, or until just cooked through and tender. Remove the chicken breasts to a cutting board and reserve.

Lightly sprinkle the sugar over the onions and garlic and continue to cook, tossing, over low heat until caramelized. Remove from the skillet and reserve.

In a large bowl, whisk the remaining ¼ cup oil with the vinegar and cloves. Season with salt and pepper.

Add the lettuce and toss lightly, just to coat. Divide the lettuce between 2 dinner plates.

Add the beans to the remaining dressing and toss. Divide between the plates.

Peel the mango and cut into very thin slices. Thinly slice the chicken on the bias. Divide between the plates, overlapping the slices.

Divide the onions and garlic between the plates. Drizzle some of the remaining vinaigrette over the chicken. Scatter the blackberries over each salad.

Serves 2

Calories: 1,244 per serving

Wine: Tavel or Domaine Ott (Rosé)

BEET GREENS AND PANCETTA

Pancetta is rolled, peppered fresh bacon with a strong pork flavor. When rendered, the bacon retains its crispy curlicue shape. Use the renderings to make the drippings that will wilt the slightly rough and bitterish greens.

Ingredients

8 ounces pancetta, cut into ¼-inch-thick slices

1 large bunch scallions, trimmed and split lengthwise

1 bunch golden beet greens, trimmed and washed

1 bunch red beet greens, trimmed and washed

1 bunch field cress or watercress, trimmed and washed

Honey Mustard Dressing

1 tablespoon honey mixed with 2 teaspoons Dijon mustard, or 1⅔ tablespoons honey mustard

½ cup olive oil

½ cup apple cider vinegar

Salt

Method

In a large skillet, cook the pancetta over moderate heat until the fat is rendered and the pancetta is browned. Drain on paper towels and set aside.

Add the scallions to the drippings and cook slowly, turning, until wilted. Remove and set aside. Reserve 2 tablespoons of the pancetta drippings.

Mix all of the greens together and arrange on 4 serving plates.

Scatter the pancetta and wilted scallions over the greens.

In a bowl, whisk together the honey and mustard with the reserved pancetta drippings. Add the oil and vinegar and season with salt to taste.

Serve the salad at room temperature and pass the dressing separately.

Serves 4

Calories: salad—128 per serving
dressing—80 per tablespoon

Wine: Beaujolais Villages (Duboeuf)

LAMB AND PEPPER SALAD WITH EGGPLANT CHIPS

This elegant salad is a hearty meal—my pulled-apart version of a ratatouille, echoing the flavors of Provence. When serving a number of people, a charcoal-grilled butterflied leg of lamb can be substituted.

Ingredients

2-pound loin of lamb, boned, trimmed, and tied

1 tablespoon fresh rosemary leaves

Salt and freshly milled black pepper

½ cup plus 2 tablespoons olive oil

1 garlic clove, crushed

4 yellow bell peppers, seeded, deveined, and cut into medium julienne

4 red bell peppers, seeded, deveined, and cut into medium julienne

¼ cup raspberry or blueberry vinegar (see page 31)

1 tablespoon Dijon mustard

8 round baby white or purple eggplants

Method

Preheat the oven to 400 degrees.

Rub the lamb with the rosemary and season with salt and pepper.

Place the lamb on a rack in a roasting pan and roast for 25 minutes. Remove the meat and set aside to cool to room temperature; set the roasting pan with drippings aside.

Meanwhile, in a large skillet, warm 2 tablespoons of the oil over moderate heat. Add the garlic and slowly sauté until golden. Remove from the skillet and set aside.

Add the yellow pepper julienne and reduce the heat to moderately low.

Cook the peppers, tossing, until wilted. Remove with tongs or a slotted spoon and reserve.

Add the red pepper julienne and cook, tossing, until wilted. Remove and set aside.

Place the roasting pan with the drippings over moderate heat and deglaze with the vinegar and mustard to make a dressing; set aside.

Slice the loin of lamb lengthwise into long, paper-thin strips.

Make the eggplant chips: With a home electric slicer or very sharp knife, cut the eggplant into paper-thin slices.

Heat the remaining ½ cup oil in a large skillet over moderate heat. Working in batches, fry the eggplant until golden brown; drain on paper towels. Season the chips with salt.

To serve, toss the yellow and red peppers together and mound them in the center of a large serving plate. Arrange the lamb, crisscrossing the slices, on top of the peppers. Surround the peppers with a ring of eggplant chips and drizzle the lamb with the dressing.

Serves 4

Calories: 423 calories per serving

Wine: Dolcetto d'Alba or Borolo

STEAK SALAD

A sublimely simple treatment for those who live by the old standby of a steak and salad diet. Here, one pound of steak with dressed greens serves two, effectively stretching the meat without stretching either your stomach or your pocket.

Ingredients

1 small head garlic

Vegetable oil

1 pound boneless sirloin steak, with fat

Salt and freshly milled black pepper

1 small hot red chile pepper, halved, seeded, and cut into julienne

1 large bunch watercress, washed and dried

1 bunch scallions, trimmed, halved crosswise, and cut into strips

Two 5-inch pieces fresh or canned hearts of palm, sliced lengthwise into thin strips

½ cup Vinaigrette (see page 35)

Method

Pull the head of garlic apart and blanch the cloves in boiling water for 5 minutes. Cool under running water and remove the skins. Drain.

In a medium skillet, heat a film of oil over moderate heat and slowly sauté the garlic until golden. Remove the cloves and set aside.

Increase the heat under the skillet to high.

Season the steak with salt and pepper and sear in the skillet for 3 to 4 minutes on each side, until lightly crusted and browned. The steak will be rare. If necessary, continue to cook to desired doneness.

In a large bowl, toss the chile pepper, watercress, scallions, and hearts of palm with the vinaigrette. Divide between 2 plates.

Trim off the fat and slice the steak into thin strips. Arrange the slices over the greens. Sprinkle with the garlic cloves.

Serve at room temperature.

Serves 2

Calories: salad—630 per serving

Wine: chilled Brouilly (Duboeuf or Château de la Chaize) or other cru Beaujolais

SAVOY CABBAGE, SMOKED HAM, AND BACON SALAD

I get a kick out of simplifying traditional dishes. Essentially this is a ten-minute *choucroute* in the form of a salad. Spiced up with hot red pepper flakes, it is hearty and perfect for a cool summer's day.

Ingredients

1 small head Savoy cabbage

4 cups chicken stock or broth

1 tablespoon dried red pepper flakes

8 ounces slab bacon, sliced

8 ounces corncob-smoked ham, cut about ¼ inch thick and trimmed of fat

¼ cup loosely packed fresh dill sprigs

Poppy Seed Dressing

1 cup olive oil

⅓ cup apple cider vinegar

2 tablespoons sugar

1 tablespoon poppy seed

1 teaspoon dry mustard

1 teaspoon salt

Method

Split the cabbage and cut it into ribbons.

In a large pot, bring the stock and red pepper flakes to a boil over high heat.

Turn off the heat and add the cabbage. Set aside for 5 minutes. Drain well and reserve the stock for another use.

Meanwhile, in a large skillet, render the bacon over moderate heat until crisp. Drain on paper towels and set aside.

Add the ham to the skillet and sauté until browned. Set aside.

Divide the cabbage among 4 plates and place the ham over it. Place strips of bacon on top and sprinkle with the dill.

In a bowl, whisk together all of the dressing ingredients.

Serve the salad at room temperature and pass the dressing separately.

Serves 4

Calories: salad—480 per serving
dressing—85 per tablespoon

Wine: Johannisberg Riesling (Jos. Phelps, Napa Valley)

CHICKEN WING SALAD

Waste not, want not—an adage the Chinese live by. We can, too—spending just a couple of bucks to serve up inexpensive, comforting food with an Oriental zing.

Ingredients

Marinade

¼ cup soy sauce

½ cup white rum

¼ cup fresh lime juice

1 tablespoon safflower oil

1 tablespoon Dijon mustard

¼ cup packed brown sugar

1-inch knob of gingerroot, peeled and very thinly sliced

1 small hot red chile pepper, cut in half (including seeds)

4 pounds chicken wings, trimmed at the second joint (use only the upper joint; reserve the lower joint for stock)

Safflower oil, to coat the skillet

1 large head salad bowl lettuce, washed and dried

1 pint red pear or cherry tomatoes

½ chayote, trimmed, sliced thin, and cut into julienne

3 to 4 cactus pears (prickly pears), peeled and sliced in ¼-inch-thick disks

Method

In a large bowl, whisk the marinade liquids with the mustard and sugar. Add the ginger and chile pepper. Add the wing-drumsticks to the marinade. Cover and refrigerate for 4 to 5 hours.

In a large skillet, heat enough oil to lightly coat the bottom of the pan over moderate heat. Remove the wings from the marinade and sauté, turning from time to time, until browned, about 10 minutes. Remove the pepper pods from the marinade and pour the marinade over the chicken. Bring to a simmer and allow the marinade to reduce and thicken slightly, about 10 minutes.

Meanwhile, divide the lettuce, tomatoes, chayote, and prickly pears among 4 plates.

Tuck the wings into the salads. Spoon the heated sauce over the salad and serve.

Serves 4

Calories: salad—350 per serving
marinade dressing—167 per serving,
40 per tablespoon

Wine: California dry rosé (Simi)

CHERYL'S DUCK SALAD WITH HUNTER'S SAUCE

What to do with a lima bean: Break the bank and go for throwaway luxury. Here, the American-raised duck breasts and *foie de canard* are luxe items imitating the best of their French cousins.

Ingredients

1 large bunch oakleaf lettuce, washed and torn into bite-size pieces

1 large head salad bowl lettuce, washed and torn into bite-size pieces

2 pounds fresh lima beans, shelled

⅔ cup plus 2 tablespoons olive oil

2 yellow bell peppers, seeded, deveined, and cut into medium julienne

2 red pimiento peppers, seeded, deveined, and cut into medium julienne

1 duck breast half (*magret*, 8- to 12-ounces), at room temperature

1 sprig fresh thyme

2 tablespoons aged balsamic vinegar

¼ teaspoon sugar

Salt and freshly milled black pepper

6 ounces fresh *foie de canard* or prepared *foie gras*

6 tablespoons unsalted butter

1 black truffle, cut into julienne

⅓ cup warm Hunter's Sauce (recipe follows)

Method

Refrigerate the greens.

In a large saucepan, gently boil the lima beans for 10 to 15 minutes, or until firm-tender.

Drain well, return the beans to the pan, and toss lightly over moderate heat to dry. Set aside.

Meanwhile, warm the 2 tablespoons oil in a large skillet over moderate heat.

Add the yellow peppers and cook, tossing, until wilted. Remove with tongs to a bowl and set aside.

Add the red peppers to the skillet and cook, tossing, until wilted. Add to the yellow peppers.

Wipe out the skillet and place over moderate heat. Rub the duck with the thyme. Place the duck skin side down in the skillet and cook until golden, about 4 minutes. Turn and sear, 2 to 3 minutes, until rare. Set aside.

In a large bowl, whisk together the remaining ⅔ cup oil with the vinegar, sugar, and salt and pepper to taste. Add the lettuces and toss to just coat. Divide the greens among 3 dinner plates.

Add the lima beans and peppers to the vinaigrette and toss. Divide among the dinner plates.

Thinly slice the duck breast and arrange the slices over the greens.

Cut the *foie de canard* into very thin slices.

In a large skillet, melt the butter over moderate heat. Working in batches, add the duck liver and sauté for about 30 seconds on each side. Divide among the plates and sprinkle with truffle julienne.

Lightly coat each slice of duck breast with Hunter's Sauce and serve the salad at room temperature.

Serves 3

Calories: 1,142 per serving

Wine: Gewürztraminer (Léon Beyer, Hugel, or Bott)

HUNTER'S SAUCE

Ingredients

2 tablespoons Harvey's Sauce (available in specialty food stores)

1 tablespoon Harvey's Mushroom Ketchup (available in specialty food stores)

Juice and grated zest of ½ lemon

3 shallots, minced

3 whole cloves

¼ teaspoon ground mace

⅛ teaspoon cayenne pepper

1½ cups chicken stock

¾ cup dry sherry

3 tablespoons unsalted butter

3 tablespoons all-purpose flour

Method

In a nonreactive saucepan, combine the Harvey's Sauce, ketchup, lemon juice and zest, shallots, cloves, mace, cayenne pepper, and stock. Bring to a boil over high heat. Reduce the heat to moderately low and cook for 10 minutes.

Add the sherry and bring to a boil. Strain into a bowl and set aside.

Knead the butter with the flour to make a thick paste (*beurre manie*).

Place the mixture in a large saucepan and cook, stirring constantly, for 2 minutes to thicken.

Off the heat, stir in the sauce mixture. Return to moderately high heat and bring to a boil. Reduce the heat to low and simmer for 5 minutes.

Makes about 1 cup

FRESH FRUIT WITH CHERRY COULIS

We've come a long way from the traditional fruit salad: We don't mix it, but keep it all separate. The cherry coulis is tart and refreshing, an elegant addition to a simple plate of seasonal fruits. With wheat bread and creamy *Robiola,* this fruit salad becomes a meal.

Ingredients

Cherry Coulis

1 quart bing cherries, stemmed and pitted

½ cup superfine sugar

¼ cup kirsch

Fruit

Any combination of:

- Raspberries
- Blackberries
- Blueberries
- Sectioned oranges
- Sliced white peaches
- Sliced yellow peaches
- Sliced plums
- Grapes

Method

In a nonreactive saucepan, combine the cherries, sugar, and kirsch. Bring to a boil over high heat. Reduce the heat to low and simmer, stirring occasionally, for 10 minutes.

Pour the mixture into a food processor or blender and puree until smooth.

Strain through a fine sieve and chill.

Attractively arrange the fruit over a large platter and pass the coulis separately. Serve with wheat kernel bread and creamy *Robiola* cheese.

Serves 4

Calories: Coulis only—260 per serving

Wine: Schramsberg Cuvée de Pinot sparkling wine

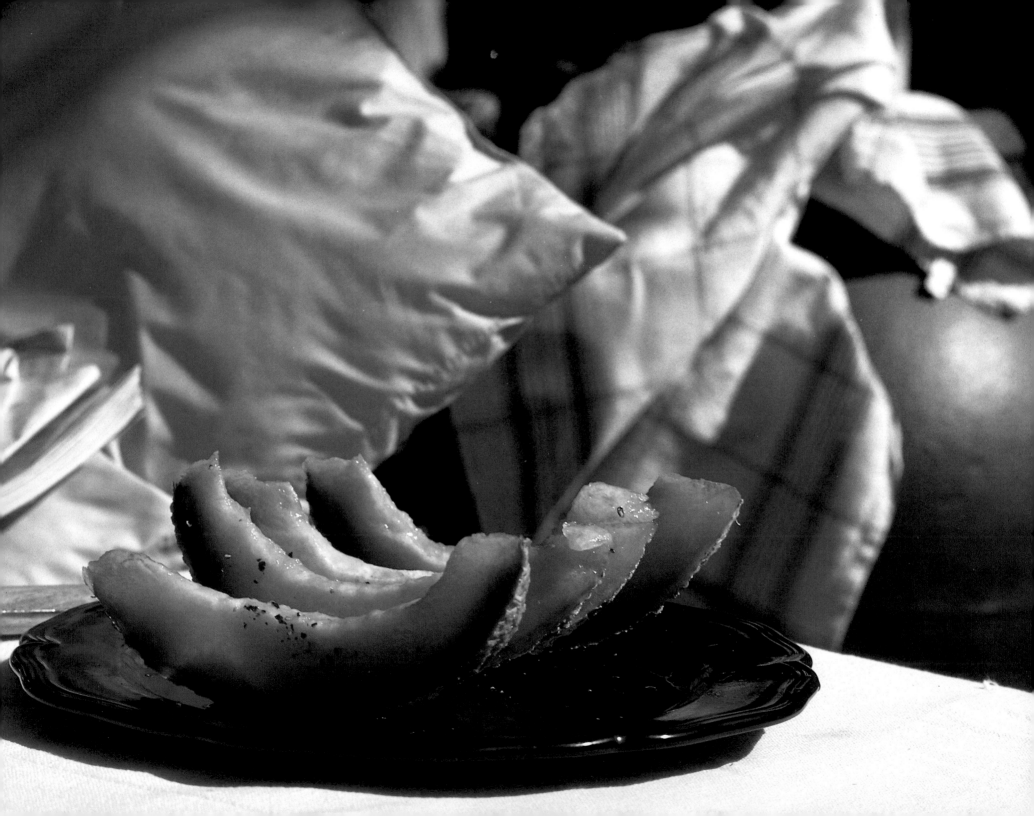

MELON WITH MADEIRA AND BLACK PEPPER

This is a summer refresher for a hot, hot day when you're too lazy to even slice off the melon rind. Eat as much as you like, and nothing else. Or serve it as a first course for a crowd.

Ingredients

2 ripe cantaloupes

¾ cup Madeira wine

2 teaspoons freshly cracked black pepper

4 sprigs fresh mint

Method

Halve the melons and discard the seeds.

Slice the melons into 1-inch-thick wedges.

Divide the wedges among 4 plates and splash with the Madeira.

Sprinkle with the pepper and serve with a mint sprig on the side.

Serves 4

Calories: 132 per serving

Wine: Bual Madeira

PROSCIUTTO AND FIGS

This tireless, classic dish is never better than when the prosciutto is rich and succulent and the figs are bursting out of their skins.

Ingredients

24 ripe figs

1 pound prosciutto, sliced paper-thin

Method

Layer the prosciutto over 4 large plates.

Cut the figs lengthwise in half and arrange them over the ham.

Serve with semolina bread and sweet butter.

Serves 4

Calories: 400 per serving

Wine: Italian Nebbiolo

BREAST OF CAPON SALAD SERVED WITH MANGO

My preference for chicken salad is white meat only. Roasted chicken or capon produces the best flavor and the cold cooked chicken makes neat cubes. Roast the capon the night before you plan to make this salad. Mango is a not-too-sweet complement to the sweet chicken, and be sure to use the feathery cilantro leaves—a hint of this herb is sufficient.

Ingredients

2 boneless skinless roasted chicken breasts or ½ capon breast, chilled

¾ cup Lime Mayonnaise (see page 36)

1 small ripe mango

2 sprigs fresh cilantro with blossoms

Method

Cut the breasts into large bite-size cubes.

Toss the chicken with enough mayonnaise to coat. Divide in half and mound the salad on one side of each dinner plate.

Cut the mango flush against the pit on each side to make two flat-cut halves.

With a sharp knife, score the fruit diagonally in two directions without piercing the skin.

Push up on the center of the skin side of the mango to make the fruit pop up and separate into cubes.

Place a cut mango on each plate and serve with a cilantro blossom on top of the capon salad.

Serves 2

Calories: 775 per serving

Wine: California Chardonnay (Jekel or Fetzer "Barrel Select")

The hot pepper, the sweet and cooling fruit, the refreshing dill, and the soothing yogurt sauce make this a nice light shrimp salad.

Ingredients

¼ cup tarragon vinegar (see page 30)

2 garlic cloves, crushed

1 small red onion, thinly sliced

½ lemon, thinly sliced

1 teaspoon dried red pepper flakes

1 pound medium shrimp, in their shells

1 cup plain yogurt

¼ cup Mayonnaise (see page 36)

1 tablespoon fresh lemon juice

2 tablespoons chopped fresh dill

1 ripe papaya, peeled and sliced into 16 wedges with a few seeds reserved

Method

In a large nonreactive pot, combine the vinegar, garlic, onion, lemon, and red pepper flakes with 4 cups of water. Bring to a boil over high heat.

Add the shrimp and cook for 3 minutes; drain immediately. Cool under cold running water.

When cool enough to handle, shell the shrimp, leaving the tail attached.

In a small bowl, stir together the yogurt, mayonnaise, lemon juice, and dill until well combined.

Divide the papaya wedges among 4 plates. Place the shrimp over the papaya and drizzle with the dressing.

Add some of the papaya seeds and serve at room temperature.

Serves 4

Calories: 286 per serving

Wine: Portuguese Vinho Verde

SEAFOOD SALAD

This is a summer feast for a crowd.

Ingredients

Stock

1 medium red onion, halved

Juice and grated zest of 1 lemon

2 garlic cloves, crushed

2 tablespoons Old Bay Seasoning

1½ cups dry white wine

2 tablespoons olive oil

2 cups cold water

Salad

24 large fresh shrimp

3 squid, cleaned and cut into rings

1 pound bay or sea scallops

1 pound black bass, snapper, or other white fish except flounder fillets, skinned

1 pound salmon fillets, skinned

1 pound tuna fillets

1 green bell pepper, seeded, deveined, and cut into fine julienne

1 red bell pepper, seeded, deveined and cut into fine julienne

1 yellow bell pepper, seeded, deveined and cut into fine julienne

Juice of 1½ limes

3 tablespoons olive oil

12 ounces salmon roe caviar

Method

In a large nonreactive pot, bring all of the stock ingredients to a boil over high heat. Reduce the heat to a simmer. Add the shrimp and cook for 2 minutes; remove immediately with tongs or a slotted spoon and drain.

Turn off the heat and add the squid to the stock. Let sit for 5 minutes. Remove with a slotted spoon and drain. Keep the stock warm.

Add the scallops to the stock and warm them for 2 to 3 minutes, or until just opaque. Remove with a slotted spoon and drain.

Cut the fish into bite-size chunks and place on a large deep platter.

Sprinkle the bell peppers over the fish.

While the stock is still warm, strain over the fish and peppers.

Set aside until the liquid has cooled to room temperature. Cover and refrigerate for 1 to 2 hours, but not longer.

To serve, drain off the stock. (Boil and freeze for another use.) Shell the shrimp, leaving the tails attached. Add the shrimp, squid, and scallops to the fish and peppers.

Add the lime juice and oil and toss to coat. Arrange the seafood on a serving platter. Mound the caviar in the center of the salad and serve.

Serves 8

Calories: 430 calories per serving
caviar—69 per serving

Wine: Chablis, Premier Cru (Davissat or Ravenneau)

SQUID SALAD

The Italian approach is the simple approach. These sweet little terrors should be cooked quickly and delicately and bathed and seasoned in the simplest way.

Ingredients

3 pounds medium squid, cleaned

About ¾ cup extra-virgin olive oil

Coarse (kosher) salt

Juice of 1 small lemon

½ cup coarsely chopped Italian parsley

Freshly milled black pepper

Method

Wash and dry the squid thoroughly. Cut the mantle into ¾-inch rings and the tentacles into bite-size pieces; if the tentacles are small, leave them whole. Dry again.

Pour about ¼ cup of the oil (or enough to measure ⅛ inch deep) into a large skillet.

Toss the squid in the oil and place the skillet over very low heat. Season with coarse salt and cook for 5 to 8 minutes, or until tender and buttery; do not overcook or the squid will toughen.

Drain the squid in a large sieve and set aside to cool to room temperature.

Place the squid in a large bowl and add the remaining ½ cup oil, the lemon juice, and parsley. Season with pepper to taste, cover, and refrigerate for about 20 minutes, or just until chilled.

Serve with crusty Italian bread.

Serves 4

Calories: 593 per serving

Wine: Pinot Grigio or Verdicchio (Jesi)

LIME-MARINATED SWORDFISH AND SQUASH SALAD

I treat the vegetables in this salad as I would fresh pasta, piling them on the plate and covering them with thin slices of fish. This tasty steak "cooks" in its own sweet marinade. A home electric slicer makes the preparation a cinch.

Ingredients

Fish and marinade

1 cup olive oil

½ cup fresh lime juice

2 tablespoons chopped fresh tarragon

1 pound boneless swordfish steak thick-cut

Freshly milled black pepper

Dressing

¼ cup mirin (Japanese cooking sauce)

2 tablespoons white wine vinegar

Juice of ½ lime

½ cup extra-virgin olive oil

Salt and freshly milled black pepper

Salad

3 pattypan squash, trimmed and thinly sliced

3 yellow squash or zucchini, trimmed and thinly sliced lengthwise

1 mild red chile pepper, seeded, deveined, and cut into long fine julienne

Method

Prepare the fish and marinade: In a bowl, whisk together the oil, lime juice, and tarragon.

Using an electric home slicer, slice the swordfish steak into thin ⅛-inch-thick sheets.

Layer the fish in a nonreactive dish, alternating with the marinade and black pepper.

Cover with plastic wrap and refrigerate for at least 2 hours, but not longer than 3 hours.

Just before serving, prepare the dressing: In a large bowl, whisk together the dressing ingredients and season with salt and pepper to taste.

Add the pattypan and yellow squashes and half of the red chile julienne. Set aside at room temperature, tossing from time to time.

To serve, turn the vegetables onto a serving plate and arrange the swordfish slices on top. Finely dice the remaining red chile julienne and sprinkle over the fish.

Serves 2

Calories: salad—373 per serving
dressing—60 per tablespoon

Wine: California Chardonnay (Shafer Vineyard)

CRABMEAT SALAD WITH HOT PEPPER ROUILLE

Crabmeat salad can be delicate or gutsy. Old Bay Seasoning gives it a punch and the hot green cherry pepper *rouille* is offset by red onion salad and cooled by the coleslaw.

Ingredients

Rouille

6 hot green cherry peppers, roasted, peeled, and seeded

3 large garlic cloves

1 tablespoon chopped cilantro

1 thin slice white bread, soaked in ¼ cup chive vinegar (see page 30) or red wine vinegar and squeezed dry

1 teaspoon Old Bay Seasoning

2 egg yolks

Finely grated zest of ¼ lemon

Juice of ½ lemon

Salt and freshly milled black pepper to taste

1 cup fruity virgin olive oil

Crabs

¼ cup distilled white vinegar

12 live blue crabs (#1 jimmies), or 2 cups lump crabmeat, picked over

½ cup Old Bay Seasoning

Method

Make the *rouille:* In a food processor or blender, combine all of the *rouille* ingredients except the olive oil. Process until smooth. Gradually add the oil and process until the *rouille* has the consistency of mayonnaise. Set aside.

Prepare the crabs: In a large steamer or stockpot, bring 2 quarts of water to a boil over high heat. Add the vinegar and a single layer of crabs. Sprinkle on one-third of the Old Bay Seasoning and add a second layer of crabs. Sprinkle on half of the remaining seasoning and add the remaining crabs. Top with the remaining seasoning. Cover and steam for 20 minutes.

Remove the crabs with tongs; remove the claws and "fingers." Lift the apron, pull off the top shell, and reserve. Trim the "knuckles" with a paring knife and split the body in half. Pick out the crabmeat.

Divide the crabmeat among the shells and spoon the *rouille* over it. (If using lump crabmeat, mound the crab on a bed of greens and coat with the *rouille.*)

Serve at once with Coleslaw and Red Onion Salad (recipes follow).

Serves 4

Calories: 143 per serving

Wine: Bandol rosé (Ott or Fregate) or beer

99

COLESLAW

Ingredients

1 small head green cabbage, coarsely shredded (about 4 cups)

1 small red bell pepper, seeded, deveined, and finely diced

1 small white onion, finely diced

Dressing

2/3 cup hot red pepper oil (see page 27)

1/3 cup chive vinegar (see page 30)

2 teaspoons sugar

1/2 cup cold water

Salt

Method

In a large bowl, toss together the cabbage, red pepper, and onion.

In a small bowl, whisk together the dressing ingredients. Season with salt to taste.

Pour the dressing over the vegetables and toss well. Refrigerate or set aside at room temperature until serving time.

Serves 4

Calories: 640 per serving

RED ONION SALAD WITH ORANGE VINAIGRETTE

Ingredients

1 large red onion, very thinly sliced

2 tablespoons chopped fresh parsley

Orange vinaigrette

2 tablespoons olive oil

2 tablespoons white wine vinegar

Juice of 1/2 orange

1/8 teaspoon ground cloves

Method

Separate the onion into rings and divide them among 4 dinner plates.

Sprinkle the parsley over the onion rings.

In a small bowl, whisk together the vinaigrette ingredients and spoon about 1 tablespoon over each serving.

Serve at room temperature.

Serves 4

Calories: 84 per serving

CLAMS WITH SALSA

These little nuggets, when steamed, make a delightful beach lunch, or, if you're deft with a knife, eat them fresh and coated with the spicy salsa. Whatever you do, mop it all up with crusty bread.

Ingredients

Salsa

3 mild red cherry peppers, seeded and deveined

1 small red chile pepper, seeded and deveined

1 small onion

2 large ripe tomatoes, quartered

2 garlic cloves

2 tablespoons fresh lime juice

Clams

1 cup dry white wine

3 tablespoons chopped cilantro

2 large garlic cloves, chopped

2 dozen clams, such as littlenecks, scrubbed

Method

Prepare the salsa: Combine all of the salsa ingredients in a food processor and chop roughly. Turn into a bowl, cover, and chill.

Prepare the clams: Place the clams in the freezer for 10 minutes. Combine the wine, cilantro, and garlic in a deep nonreactive pot and bring to a boil over high heat. Add the clams, cover, and steam. As the clams open, remove them to a bowl. Discard any that do not open.

Reduce the cooking liquid by half over high heat.

Strain the liquid and allow it to cool. Add to the salsa, pour over the clams, and toss well.

Serve at room temperature.

Serves 2

Calories: 321 per serving

Wine: Beer or Ventana Pinot Blanc

GIGI SALAD

This salad was inspired by a Palm restaurant special. Make it for two or 20—you'll have a great main course.

Ingredients

6 slices smoked lean bacon

8 ounces medium shrimp, in their shells

1 pound green beans, trimmed and cut into 1-inch lengths

¼ cup plus 2 tablespoons extra-virgin olive oil

¼ cup safflower oil

Juice and grated zest of 1 lemon

1 teaspoon fresh tarragon leaves, or ¼ teaspoon dried

Salt and freshly milled white pepper

2 medium tomatoes, seeded and cut into bite-size chunks

1 medium onion, cut into medium dice

2 tablespoons chopped fresh parsley

Freshly cracked white pepper

Method

In a large skillet, render the bacon over moderately low heat until crisp and golden. Drain on paper towels. When cool, roughly chop and set aside.

Meanwhile, cook the shrimp in lightly salted boiling water for 2 to 3 minutes, or until just tender. Do not overcook. Drain and cool under cold running water.

Shell the shrimp, leaving the tail attached. Set aside.

In a pot of lightly salted boiling water, cook the beans until tender. Refresh under cold running water and drain well.

Make the vinaigrette: In a large bowl, whisk together the oils, lemon juice and zest, and tarragon. Season with salt and pepper to taste.

Add the bacon, shrimp, beans, tomatoes, onion, and parsley and toss to coat very well.

Divide the salad between 2 plates, and sprinkle with cracked pepper. Serve at room temperature.

Serves 2

Calories: salad—349 per serving
dressing—110 per tablespoon

Wine: California Chenin Blanc (Chappellet)

ARMAGNAC-MARINATED SALMON AND SNAPPER

Salmon and snapper are delicate fish that may be eaten raw, as the Japanese prefer, or "cooked" in a marinade. This marinade, with its hint of clove, does nothing more than gently "warm" the fish.

105

Ingredients

Marinated Fish

1 pound salmon fillets, with skin attached

1 pound snapper, monkfish, or other white-fleshed fish (except sole) fillets, with skin attached

¼ cup olive oil

¼ to ½ teaspoon ground cloves

1 to 1½ tablespoons Armagnac

1 lemon, thinly sliced

Tarragon Vinaigrette

½ cup extra-virgin olive oil

¼ cup tarragon wine vinegar (see page 30)

¼ cup Armagnac

Salt and freshly milled black pepper

Vegetables

8 ounces shelled fresh cranberry beans, cooked until tender in lightly salted boiling water, drained and cooled

2 small globe zucchini or regular zucchini, trimmed, seeded, and cut into julienne

4 large red radishes, trimmed and cut into julienne

1 tablespoon chopped fresh chervil

Method

Marinate the fish: Place the salmon and snapper fillets, skin side down, in a single layer in a shallow nonreactive dish. Coat the fish with the olive oil (or more if needed) and sprinkle sparingly with the cloves. Drizzle with the Armagnac and cover with the lemon slices. Cover tightly with plastic wrap and refrigerate for 2 to 3 hours.

When ready to prepare the dish, make the vinaigrette: In a large bowl, whisk together the oil, vinegar, and Armagnac. Season with salt and pepper to taste.

Add the vegetables and chervil to the vinaigrette and toss to mix well. Set aside at room temperature, tossing from time to time.

To serve, slice the fish into paper-thin slices, cutting against the skin, as you would slice smoked salmon.

Alternate slices of the two fish on 4 individual plates, overlapping slightly. Divide the vegetables among the plates.

Serve at room temperature with crusty light wheat bread and sweet butter.

Serves 4 as a main course or 6 as a first course

Calories: 4 servings—salad/436 per serving
marinade/145 per serving
6 servings—salad/290 per serving
marinade/97 per serving
dressing: 107 per tablespoon

Wine: Chassagne-Montrachet

LOBSTER SALAD WITH CORAL MAYONNAISE

The smaller the lobster, the easier it is to handle. This crustacean seems too beautiful and too expensive to hack up into a salad so I present it whole. The coral from the lobster enriches the mayonnaise with lobster flavor.

Ingredients

4 female lobsters, each about 1½ pounds

2 egg yolks, at room temperature

1 cup olive oil

2 teaspoons fresh lemon juice

Grated zest of ¼ lemon

1 teaspoon Dijon mustard

1 teaspoon boiling water

Salt

Cayenne pepper

Reserved coral from the lobsters, or ½ teaspoon chopped fresh tarragon

Method

Plunge the lobsters into a large pot of salted boiling water and cook for 14 minutes. Remove and chill.

Using poultry shears, cut away the shell and remove the tail meat in one piece.

Crack the claws and remove the meat in one piece. Wrap both kinds of meat in plastic and refrigerate.

Pick out any remaining meat and set aside, along with the coral.

Make the mayonnaise: In a food processor or blender, beat the egg yolks until thick. Add the oil in a thin steady stream and process until emulsified. Add the lemon juice and zest, and the mustard; beat until creamy. Blend in the boiling water and season with salt and cayenne to taste. Add the coral and beat until smooth. Stir enough of the mayonnaise into the reserved bits to coat lightly. Cover separately and chill.

To serve, slice the tail meat into ¼-inch medallions and arrange on each plate. Add the claw meat and a pool of the coral mayonnaise.

Serves 4

Calories: lobster—160 per serving
mayonnaise—130 per tablespoon

Wine: Puligny-Montrachet or Champagne

Fresh tender shrimp can be eaten shell and all. If this does not appeal to you, peel them. I like throwing everything into one pot and sousing the corn with good shrimp flavor.

Ingredients

1 cup dry white wine

4 ears fresh sweet corn, cut off the cobs (about 2 cups)

16 medium shrimp, in their shells

¼ cup hot red pepper oil (see page 27)

1 red chile pepper, seeded, deveined, and cut into fine julienne

1 jalapeño pepper, seeded, deveined, and cut into fine julienne

2 scallions, cut into thin rounds (including 2 inches of the green)

1 tablespoon whole cilantro leaves

Method

Pour the wine into a large nonreactive saucepan and bring to a simmer over moderate heat.

Add the corn and shrimp and simmer until the shrimp turn pink and the corn is heated through. Remove the corn and shrimp with a slotted spoon and chill.

Add the oil to the cooking liquid and whisk thoroughly to make a dressing. Set aside to cool to room temperature.

Toss the corn and shrimp with the dressing. Fold in the peppers and scallions and sprinkle with the cilantro. Serve at room temperature.

Serves 2

Calories: 495 per serving

Wine: Dry Muscat (Alsace)

Any smoked fish will benefit from this creamy blue cheese dressing, though I particularly like it with smoked sturgeon. It's equally good over roasted new potatoes or in a just-split baked potato.

Ingredients

Dressing

⅓ cup sour cream

2 ounces blue cheese, crumbled and at room temperature

1½ teaspoons dry white wine

1 teaspoon capers, drained

1 teaspoon prepared horseradish, drained

Grated zest of ½ lemon

2 teaspoons snipped fresh chives

Salad

1 large bunch watercress

8 ounces smoked sturgeon, thinly sliced

2 large thin slices red onion, separated into rings

5 shoots fresh chives, snipped

Method

In a food processor or blender, combine all of the dressing ingredients and process until creamy and smooth.

Wash and dry the watercress. Arrange it on a serving platter and place the slices of sturgeon over the top. Scatter with the onion rings and sprinkle with the chives.

Drizzle some of the dressing over the salad and serve. Serve the remainder of the dressing separately.

Serves 2

Calories: 689 per serving

Wine: Oregon Pinot Gris (Eyrie) or California Fumé Blanc

CEVICHE

Ceviché is an easy dish to prepare, usually made with fresh whitefish or conch, though I prefer it with scallops. The addition of vegetables makes for a more robust yet traditional salad.

Ingredients

1 pound bay or sea scallops (see Note)

⅓ cup fresh lime juice

2 tablespoons olive oil

Pinch of ground cloves

1 tablespoon chopped cilantro

1 pound sugar snap peas, trimmed

½ red bell pepper, seeded, deveined, and cut into julienne

½ cup Vinaigrette (see page 35)

Method

In a medium bowl, combine the scallops with the lime juice, oil, cloves, and cilantro. Cover and refrigerate for at least 2 hours.

Cook the peas in lightly salted boiling water for 5 minutes, or until tender. Drain and cool under cold running water; then drain again.

In a bowl, combine the snap peas with the bell pepper and toss with enough vinaigrette to coat. Cover and refrigerate until chilled.

Divide the *ceviché* and snap pea salad between the chilled plates and serve.

Serves 3 to 4

Note: Fresh scallops should not be washed.

Calories: for 4—285 per serving
for 3—380 per serving

Wine: Acacia or Edna Valley Chardonnay

SUNSET SALAD

Make this salad when summer is ending and the garden is ablaze with golden vegetables and fruits—a farewell before the frost.

Ingredients

1 pint yellow cherry tomatoes

2 large yellow tomatoes, seeded and cubed

4 ripe red plum tomatoes, halved

8 small golden beets, cooked, peeled, and thinly sliced

8 small red beets, cooked, peeled, and thinly sliced

1 bunch baby finger carrots, trimmed with ½ inch of the greens attached and scraped

2 golden frying peppers, seeded, deveined, and cut into medium julienne

2 red frying peppers, seeded, deveined, and cut into medium julienne

4 golden plums, halved, pitted, and sliced

1 small bunch seedless red grapes, trimmed into 4 small clusters

2 red Bartlett pears, cored and thinly sliced

2 tangelos, peeled and sectioned

1 pound smoked salmon, thinly sliced

Walnut Vinaigrette

½ cup vegetable oil

¼ cup walnut oil

¼ cup white wine vinegar

Juice of 1 lime

Salt and freshly milled black pepper

Toasted Walnuts

2 tablespoons safflower oil

1 garlic clove

¼ cup walnut pieces

Salt

Method

Attractively arrange separate groups of the vegetables and fruits on 4 chilled plates.

Layer the salmon in the center of the platter.

In a bowl, whisk together the vinaigrette ingredients and season with salt and pepper to taste.

To toast the walnuts, warm the safflower oil in a small skillet over moderate heat.

Slowly cook the garlic until golden brown. Remove and discard.

Add the walnuts and toast, shaking the pan, until browned.

Remove at once and drain on paper towels. Sprinkle liberally with salt.

Serve the salad at room temperature with the salad dressing and toasted walnuts on the side.

Serves 4

Calories: salad—500 per serving
dressing—91 per tablespoon
walnuts—80 per serving

Wine: Sauvignon Blanc (Arbor Creek or Parducci)

WILD RICE AND VEGETABLE SALAD

This nutty and crunchy salad combines the end of fall's harvest with the durable standbys of the winter larder. The sweet red pepper puree is a rich accompaniment to this vegetarian meal.

Ingredients

2 tablespoons olive oil

Juice of ½ lemon

Salt and freshly milled black pepper

1¾ cups cooked wild rice

2 to 3 medium kohlrabi bulbs, trimmed, peeled, halved lengthwise, sliced ¼-inch-thick, and steamed until crisp-tender

8 finger carrots, scraped, halved lengthwise, and steamed until crisp-tender

4 small leeks, washed, trimmed, and cut into julienne

½ cup cranberries, washed and drained

24 walnut halves

Sauce

3 tablespoons olive oil

3 sweet red frying peppers, seeded, deveined, and coarsely chopped

1 cup packed basil leaves

Salt and freshly milled black pepper

Method

In a large bowl, whisk together the oil, lemon juice, and salt and pepper to taste. Add the wild rice, kohlrabi, carrots, leeks, cranberries, and walnuts. Toss to coat lightly. Set aside.

To make the sauce, warm 1 tablespoon of the oil in a large skillet over moderate heat. Add the peppers and sauté until wilted.

In a food processor, combine the peppers, their cooking oil, and the basil. Process, pulsing on and off, until coarsely chopped. Season with salt and pepper to taste. With the machine running, slowly add the remaining 2 tablespoons oil and process until smooth.

Divide the salad among 4 plates. Spoon some of the sauce over each salad and serve.

Serves 4

Calories: 310 per serving

Wine: Dry Pinot Blanc from Alsace or Oregon

WILD MUSHROOM SALAD

For me, eating a platter of sautéed or grilled mushrooms is as satisfying as a good steak. No matter what the variety, wild mushrooms should be firm and springy to the touch. The sooner they are prepared, the better the taste.

Ingredients

1 pound fresh wild mushrooms (*pleurottes, shiitake, porcini*)

¼ cup olive oil

1 teaspoon fresh thyme leaves

Salt and freshly milled black pepper

Juice of ½ large lemon

Coarsely chopped Italian parsley, for serving

Method

Carefully wipe away any grit from the mushrooms with a damp paper towel or a mushroom brush.

If large, cut the mushrooms into halves or quarters.

In a large skillet, warm the oil over moderate heat. Add the mushrooms and thyme and cook for 4 to 5 minutes, or until the mushrooms give up their moisture and it evaporates.

Lightly season the mushrooms with salt and pepper.

Place the mushrooms in a serving dish and squeeze the lemon juice over them. Sprinkle with the parsley and serve.

Serves 2

Calories: 316 per serving

Wine: American Pinot Noir

GRILLED WINTER VEGETABLE SALAD

Although these vegetables can be cooked under a broiler or salamander or in the flames of a gas cooktop, the best flavor comes from charring them over hot coals. The lightly melted cheese and toasted pine nuts combine with the vegetables to make this a hearty rustic supper.

Ingredients

4 small eggplants

Coarse (kosher) salt

2 to 3 medium fennel bulbs

½ lemon

2 heads radicchio, halved and each half cut into thirds

3 tablespoons olive oil

Freshly milled black pepper

6 small chocolate or green bell peppers, halved, seeded, and deveined

12 store-bought mozzarella *bocconcini* (marinated in olive oil with dried red pepper flakes)

⅓ cup toasted pine nuts

½ cup chopped fresh parsley

Extra-virgin olive oil, balsamic vinegar, and lemon wedges, for serving

Method

Prepare a charcoal fire and set a large rack over the grill.

Keeping the eggplants intact at the stem ends, cut each one lengthwise into ½-inch-thick slices. Sprinkle with salt and set aside to "sweat" for 15 to 20 minutes. Dry well with paper towels, squeezing out the excess moisture.

Trim the stalks from the fennel bulbs; discard the stalks. Cut the bulbs in half and then into thirds or quarters, depending on their size.

In a large saucepan of lightly salted boiling water, squeeze the lemon to release its juice and add the lemon half. Add the fennel and cook for 3 minutes. Remove with a slotted spoon and cool under cold running water; drain thoroughly.

Add the radicchio to the cooking water and simmer for 1 minute. Remove and drain.

Brush all of the vegetables with the olive oil. Sprinkle with salt and pepper.

When the coals are ash-covered and glowing, brush the grill with oil and arrange the eggplants in the center. Surrounding the eggplants, arrange the fennel, radicchio, and peppers, cut sides up. As the vegetables brown and soften, fan out the eggplants slices.

When the vegetables are lightly charred and wilted on one side, turn over all but the peppers and grill for about 7 minutes longer.

Place a *bocconcini* in the well of each pepper. Cover the grill and cook for 7 minutes, or until the cheese melts.

Arrange the vegetables on a heated platter. Sprinkle with the pine nuts and parsley.

Serve, accompanied with olive oil, balsamic vinegar, and lemon wedges.

Serves 6

Calories: 430 per serving

Wine: Dolcetto d'Alba

MAGGIE'S PEAR SALAD

Cheese complements fruit. Roquefort is an especially excellent pairing with the proverbial pear. Poaching the pears in the Muscat adds to their fruitiness. The addition of the Parmesan is the inspiration of a friend. This dish makes a delicious light luncheon dish—and certainly would and could be salad and dessert in one at the end of a fancy meal!

Ingredients

Juice and grated zest of 1 lemon plus 1 tablespoon fresh lemon juice

½ cup sugar

10 white peppercorns, crushed

1½ cups sweet Muscat or Sauternes wine

4 small pears, peeled with stems intact and rubbed with lemon juice

¼ teaspoon salt

⅛ teaspoon freshly milled white pepper

3 tablespoons extra-virgin olive oil

1 head curly endive, torn into bite-size pieces, washed, and dried

1 Belgian endive, separated and cut crosswise into ½-inch lengths

4 ounces Roquefort cheese, cut into thin strips with a wire cheese cutter

4 ounces Parmesan cheese

Method

In a nonreactive medium saucepan, combine the lemon juice and grated zest of 1 lemon, the sugar, peppercorns, and wine. Place the pears in the mixture and add enough cold water to cover.

Bring to a boil over high heat. Reduce the heat to low and poach until the pears are tender and can be easily pierced with a knife, 15 to 20 minutes.

Remove from the heat and set aside to cool in the cooking liquid to room temperature. (The poaching should be done several hours in advance.)

To serve, remove the pears to a plate. Boil the pear cooking liquid until reduced by three-fourths.

Pour the liquid into a bowl and whisk in the remaining 1 tablespoon lemon juice, the salt, pepper, and oil to make a dressing.

Toss the salad greens with the dressing to coat lightly. Divide the greens among 4 chilled plates.

Place the Roquefort over each salad and arrange a pear on top of it. Grate the Parmesan directly over the pear with a Mouli rotary grater. Serve.

Serves 4

Calories: salad—470 per serving
Parmesan cheese—23 per tablespoon, grated

Wine: Sweet California Muscat or Sauternes

GOAT CHEESE AND ARUGULA SALAD

These bitter greens are sweetened by the balsamic dressing and the caramelized onions. When broiled or baked, rounds of good creamy goat cheese puffs up like little soufflés.

Ingredients

16 small white onions

2 tablespoons unsalted butter

2 tablespoons sugar

6 slices French bread, cut ¾ inch thick

2 tablespoons olive oil

4-ounce log creamy semisoft goat cheese, cut into 6 rounds

1 teaspoon fresh rosemary leaves, or ½ teaspoon dried

1 teaspoon fresh thyme leaves, or ½ teaspoon dried

2 bunches arugula, washed and dried

Vinaigrette (see page 35), made with balsamic vinegar

Method

In a pot of lightly salted boiling water, simmer the onions for about 7 minutes, or until tender.

Cool under running water. Carefully slip off the outer skins and pinch off the root ends; drain.

Melt the butter in a small skillet over low heat. Add the sugar and stir until melted. Add the onions and cook, tossing constantly, until the onions are well coated and caramelized. Reserve and keep warm.

Preheat the broiler.

Brush one side of each slice of bread with the olive oil. Place a round of the goat cheese on each slice. Sprinkle each disk of cheese with the herbs.

Place the bread on a baking sheet and broil until the edges of the bread are golden and the cheese is puffed.

Toss the arugula with enough vinaigrette to coat lightly. Divide between 2 plates. Place 3 slices of bread and 8 onions on each plate. Serve at once.

Serves 2

Calories: 800 per serving (using ¼ cup vinaigrette)

Wine: Sauvignon Blanc

CAESAR SALAD

This tired old chestnut of a dish can be a sublime concoction when made with care. It does not require the fanfare of preparation at the side of the dining table. I think of it as a one-dish supper menu and prefer leaving the tender small romaine leaves whole and attacking the plate with knife and fork.

Ingredients

3 garlic cloves, crushed

1 cup fruity extra-virgin olive oil

2 small baguettes French bread

3 small heads romaine lettuce, washed and dried

½ teaspoon salt (or to taste)

¼ teaspoon dry mustard

Freshly milled black pepper

5 anchovy fillets, chopped

Worcestershire sauce

2 coddled eggs (boiled for 1½ minutes, until very soft)

Juice of 1 large lemon

6 ounces Parmesan cheese

Method

Steep the garlic in the oil for 24 hours; discard the garlic.

Preheat the broiler.

Halve the baguettes lengthwise. Split each half lengthwise and then split each quarter lengthwise to make a total of 16 long thin sticks.

Brush each stick of bread with a liberal amount of the flavored olive oil. Broil, turning, as necessary, until evenly browned and golden on all sides. Set aside.

Tear the romaine into bite-size pieces, leaving the small leaves intact. Place the greens in a large salad bowl.

Sprinkle on the salt, dry mustard and a generous amount of pepper. Sprinkle on the anchovies and a few drops of Worcestershire sauce. Drizzle with ½ cup of the garlic oil.

Crack the eggs and drop them over the greens. Sprinkle on the lemon juice. Toss the salad very well to combine all of the ingredients.

Divide the greens among 4 dinner plates. Square off each plate with 4 sticks of the long "croutons."

Use a Mouli rotary grater to grate a generous amount of the Parmesan over each portion. Serve.

Serves 4

Calories: 1028 per serving (using 1 cup oil)
863 per serving (using ⅔ cup oil)

Wine: Medium-bodied Chardonnay or Cabernet Sauvignon

CURRY FRUITS WITH CHICKEN THIGHS

The fruit in this recipe is treated like a chutney, and the lettuce should still be crunchy when removed from the pan. The tender chicken thighs complete this subtle Oriental-flavored dish.

Ingredients

4 tablespoons unsalted butter

2 tablespoons curry powder

8 chicken thighs, boned

1-inch knob fresh gingerroot, peeled and grated

1 ugli fruit

1 pink honeydew melon, peel removed and the flesh cut into ¼-inch crescents

1 winter melon, peel removed and the flesh cut into ½-inch cubes

1 ruby red grapefruit, peeled and sectioned

8 dates

8 mint leaves, torn into small pieces

1 head romaine lettuce, pale green only, washed and leaves cut into ½-inch pieces

Salt and freshly milled white pepper

1 bunch fresh chives

Method

Melt 2 tablespoons of the butter in a large heavy skillet over moderately high heat.

Pat the curry powder into the chicken skin. Place the thighs in the skillet, skin side down. Sprinkle with half of the ginger.

Reduce the heat to moderately low and simmer for 5 minutes on each side, or until cooked through. Remove the thighs to a plate; set aside and keep warm.

Strain the butter and curry powder mixture into a clean nonstick skillet. Add the remaining 2 tablespoons butter.

Squeeze the ugli fruit juice into the skillet. Add the melons, grapefruit, and dates. Sprinkle on the remaining ginger and the mint leaves.

Cover and simmer for 5 to 7 minutes, or until the fruits are warmed through and begin to "sweat."

Using a slotted spatula, remove the fruits to a plate.

Add the romaine to the skillet and toss in the butter and curry. Season with salt and pepper to taste.

Divide the greens among 4 serving plates. Arrange the fruits on top of the lettuce. Slice the thighs and place on top of the fruits. Scatter several chives over each salad and serve warm.

Serves 4

Calories: 665 per serving

Wine: Dry Riesling

CHICORY, ROQUEFORT, AND PEAR SALAD

This salad has been the traditional introduction to many a French bistro meal. Usually served wilted, the dressing is made from bacon drippings, but this salad is just as enriching without the addition of all that grease.

Ingredients

1 large head white chicory (*frisée*), washed and dried

8 ounces slab bacon, sliced ¼ inch thick and then into ½-inch pieces

1 cup walnut halves

1 large ripe pear

1 tablespoon fresh lemon juice

¼ cup white wine vinegar

1 tablespoon Dijon mustard

Salt and freshly milled black pepper

½ cup vegetable oil

2 tablespoons walnut oil

8 ounces Roquefort cheese, crumbled and at room temperature

Method

Tear the chicory into bite-size pieces. Place in a large salad bowl.

In a small skillet, render the bacon until crisp and golden over moderate heat. Drain on paper towels.

Spoon 1 tablespoon of the bacon drippings into a clean skillet. Add the walnuts and toast over low heat until just slightly darkened. Drain on paper towels.

Peel the pear and cut it into ½-inch cubes.

Place the cubes in a small bowl and toss with the lemon juice.

To make the dressing, whisk together the vinegar, mustard, and salt and pepper to taste in a small bowl. Slowly add the oils and whisk until emulsified.

Pour the dressing over the chicory and toss to coat well. Sprinkle on the bacon, walnuts, pear, and Roquefort. Toss lightly and serve.

Serves 4

Calories: 770 per serving

Wine: Sancerre or Beaujolais Villages

A quick plunge into hot water removes the bitterness and softens these tart greens.

Ingredients

8 ounces slab bacon, cut in ¼-inch cubes

1 bunch broccoli raab, trimmed

1 bunch watercress, washed and trimmed

3 medium leeks, washed and cut into julienne

1 cup dry red wine.

2 teaspoons tarragon vinegar (see page 30)

¼ cup chopped shallots

¼ pound plus 1 tablespoon unsalted butter, cut into bits and chilled

Salt and freshly milled white pepper

4 slices French bread, cut 1 inch thick

4 eggs

3 tablespoons melted unsalted butter

Method

In a large skillet over moderate heat, render the bacon until crisp and golden. Drain on paper towels. Reserve 2 tablespoons of the bacon drippings.

In a steamer, steam the broccoli raab for about 5 minutes, or until the stalks wilt and are almost tender. Reserve and keep warm.

In the same steamer, steam the watercress for about 2 minutes, or until just wilted. Reserve and keep warm.

In a saucepan, blanch the leek julienne for about 1 minute. Cool under cold running water; drain.

To make the wine butter, combine the wine, 1 teaspoon of the vinegar, and the shallots in a nonreactive saucepan. Bring to a boil and reduce until the mixture becomes a glaze.

Remove from the heat and strain the glaze into another pan.

Whisk in about 2 tablespoons of the cold butter. Return to low heat and whisk in the remaining cold butter, a little bit at a time, until thickened and smooth. Season with salt and pepper to taste. Reserve and keep warm.

Brush both sides of each slice of bread with the reserved bacon drippings. In a skillet, toast the bread lightly on both sides until just golden. Reserve.

Stir the remaining 1 teaspoon vinegar into a pan of simmering water. Poach the eggs. Drain well.

In a large skillet, warm the melted butter over moderate heat. Add the broccoli raab and toss. Divide between 2 warmed dinner plates.

Add the watercress and warm in the butter. Divide between the plates.

Add the leek julienne to the butter and warm through. Divide between the plates and sprinkle on the bacon. Place 2 slices of the toast on each plate. Place a poached egg on each slice of bread.

Spoon some of the wine butter over eggs and serve.

Serves 2 as a main course or 4 as a first course

Calories: for 2—1,166 per serving
for 4—583 per serving

Wine: Light Red (Dolcetto d'Alba or Côtes du Rhône Villages)

COLD LAMB, FLAGEOLET, AND CULL SALAD

Leftover roasts have always translated into wonderful salads. I prefer making the vegetables from scratch rather than using what was leftover from last night's dinner.

Ingredients

1 pound dried flageolets, soaked overnight in water to cover, or 2 jars (15 ounces) flageolets, washed and drained

6 cups lamb or chicken stock

12 ounces large pearl onions

1 pound culls or baby new potatoes

1 to 1½ pounds roasted leg of lamb

1 teaspoon chopped fresh rosemary

1 garlic clove, minced

Vinaigrette (see page 35), made with balsamic vinegar

Salt and freshly milled black pepper

12 nasturtium flowers

Method

Drain the flageolets and discard their soaking water. Place in a saucepan with the stock and bring to a simmer over moderate heat. Cover and cook for about 1 hour, or until the beans are tender. (If using beans from jars, set aside.)

Meanwhile, with a sharp paring knife, cut an X in the root end of each onion.

In a pot of lightly salted boiling water, cook the onions for 7 to 10 minutes, until tender. Cool under cold running water. Slip off the skins and pinch off the root ends. Set aside.

In another pot of lightly salted boiling water, cook the potatoes until done. Cool under cold running water. When cool enough to handle, cut into ¼-inch slices (with or without their jackets). Set aside.

Trim the lamb of all fat and gristle. Cut the meat into ¾-inch cubes.

Drain the flageolets. Place in a large bowl along with the onions, potatoes, rosemary, and garlic. Pour on the vinaigrette and toss; season and salt and pepper to taste. Set aside for 30 minutes.

When ready to serve the salad, add the lamb and toss.

Divide the salad among 4 dinner plates. Sprinkle the nasturtium petals over the salad and serve.

Serves 4

Calories: 635 per serving (using ½ cup vinaigrette)

Wine: Beaujolais Villages or Morgan

PAN-FRIED QUAIL WITH QUINCE, APPLES, AND CABBAGE

Warm salads have enormous appeal in winter. In this one, the cruciferous cabbage is filled with nourishment and is used as a nest for the juniper-flavored quail.

Ingredients

4 quail (about 9 ounces each)

1 tablespoon Dijon mustard

1 garlic clove, minced

6 juniper berries, bruised

1 teaspoon freshly milled black pepper

Coarse (kosher) salt

½ small head white cabbage, cored and sliced ½-inch thick

1 tablespoon unsalted butter

1 quince, peeled, cored, and sliced

1 tart apple, peeled, cored, and sliced

2 tablespoons gin

½ cup Vinaigrette (see page 35), made with a fruit vinegar, such as cherry, blueberry, blackberry, or raspberry

Method

With a sharp knife, cut away the backbone of each quail. Press the birds flat, skin sides down, and carefully cut away the breast bones.

In a small bowl, combine the mustard, garlic, juniper berries, pepper, and salt to taste.

Rub the mixture evenly over both sides of the quail. Place in a bowl, cover, and refrigerate until ready to cook, about 4 hours.

If using a grill, prepare a fire. If broiling, preheat the broiler.

In a pot of lightly salted boiling water, blanch the cabbage for 1 minute. Drain in a colander; reserve.

In a nonstick skillet, melt the butter over moderate heat. Add the quince slices and sauté for about 5 minutes. Add the apple slices and sauté until all of the fruit is golden on both sides. Set aside and keep warm.

When the charcoals are glowing and ash-covered, oil the rack. Place the quails, skin side down, on the grill. Cook for 5 minutes in one side; turn and cook for 3 to 5 minutes on the other side. Splash the birds with the gin and remove from the heat when the flames have gone out.

If broiling, place the birds on a broiler pan 4 inches from the heat. Broil for about 4 minutes. Turn and cook the other side for 3 to 5 minutes. Remove the pan from the broiler and splash the quail with the gin. Ignite with a match and stand aside until the flames subside.

Toss the cabbage with the vinaigrette. Divide between 2 dinner plates.

Arrange the apple and quince slices on opposite sides of each plate and place the quail over the cabbage. Serve immediately.

Serves 2

Calories: 685 per serving

Wine: Alexander Valley Zinfandel or Red Hermitage

SWISS SALAD

Fennel adapts itself to many forms of cooking and every part is edible: the bulb, leaves, stems, seeds, and the flowers. Its sweet anise flavor is widely favored in Italy and France and is finally attracting fans in the United States. When thinly sliced, the raw flavor is crisp and delicious. This refreshing salad was served to me in a little ski hut in the Swiss Alps.

Ingredients

2 medium fennel bulbs, trimmed, reserving some of the feathery leaves

Juice of ½ lemon

1 large tart apple, peeled, cored, and thinly sliced

4 ounces *bündnerfleisch* or prosciutto, thinly sliced

⅓ cup walnuts

½ cup Mayonnaise (see page 36)

½ cup plain yogurt

¼ cup heavy cream, whipped

Freshly milled white pepper

Method

Using an electric home slicer or sharp knife, cut the fennel bulb into thin sheets.

Place the fennel in a large bowl and toss with the lemon juice. Add the apple slices and toss to coat with the lemon juice.

If using prosciutto, trim away all fat. Cut the meat into ½-inch ribbons. Add to the bowl and toss well. Sprinkle with the walnuts.

In another bowl, combine the mayonnaise with the yogurt. Fold in the whipped cream.

Fold the dressing into the salad, tossing well to coat the ingredients. Season with pepper to taste. Cover and refrigerate until chilled, about 1 hour.

To serve, roughly chop about 2 tablespoons of the reserved fennel leaves.

Divide the salad between 2 dinner plates and sprinkle with some of the chopped fennel. Serve.

Serves 2

Calories: 964 per serving

Wine: Dry Reisling

HAM SALAD

The better the ham, the better the salad. Although we tend to use the leftover ham for salads, sandwiches, and the like, a fine baked ham made just for a salad is a great way to feed a large and hungry crowd.

Ingredients

2 pounds cooked cured ham, trimmed of all fat, sliced ⅓ inch thick, and then cut into 1-inch lengths

½ cup chopped sweet pickles

1 small onion, minced

2 tablespoons chopped chives

1 cup Mayonnaise (see page 36)

Method

In a large bowl, combine the ham, pickles, onion, and chives. Fold in the mayonnaise until well blended.

Cover and refrigerate until chilled.

Serve on thick-sliced black bread.

Serves 5 to 6

Calories: for 5—828 per serving
for 6—690 per serving

Wine: hot spiced red wine or mulled cider

BEAN AND SAUSAGE SALAD

The pairing of legumes with sausages is as common in Italian dishes as it is in a French *cassoulet.* Cured sausages and beans make a nourishing wintertime supper.

Ingredients

8 ounces dried kidney beans

8 ounces dried white pea or navy beans

2 quarts chicken stock

3 jalapeño peppers, halved crosswise

3 garlic cloves

1 medium onion, halved

1 teaspoon dried thyme

1 hot red chile pepper

½ pint red pearl onions, or 1 medium red onion

¾ cup Vinaigrette (see page 35)

¼ cup chopped dill

Salt and freshly milled black pepper

1 pound cured Italian or French hard sausage, thinly sliced

Method

Wash and pick over each type of beans, keeping them separate.

Place each type of bean in a saucepan and divide the stock between them. Add water, if necessary, to cover by 2 inches.

Place 2 jalapeño halves in each pan of beans.

Crush and peel 2 of the garlic cloves. Add 1 to each pot.

Add ½ of the onion to each pot, along with half of the thyme.

Bring both pots to a boil over high heat. Reduce the heat to a simmer and cook for 45 minutes, or until the beans are tender.

Remove from the heat and let the beans cool in their liquid.

When cool, drain the beans and discard the garlic, onion, and jalapeños. Combine the beans in a large bowl.

Remove the stems and seeds from the remaining jalapeño and the red chile. Cut into fine dice. Mince the remaining garlic clove. Add all of the diced peppers and the garlic to the beans.

Thinly slice the pearl onions. Separate them into rings and add to the beans.

Fold in the vinaigrette and dill. Season with salt and pepper to taste.

Cover the beans and refrigerate for at least 4 hours, or overnight.

Let the beans warm to room temperature for 1 hour before serving.

Toss the beans well. Divide among 5 or 6 dinner plates. Arrange about 6 slices of sausage around each plate. Serve.

Serves 5 or 6

Calories: for 5—970 per serving
for 6—810 per serving

Wine: Côte Rôtie

CHICKEN SALAD WITH ROOT VEGETABLES

A good chicken salad is best dressed with mayonnaise. The root vegetables are best tossed with vinaigrette, making the combination just right for this cold *pot au feu.*

Ingredients

4½- to 5-pound chicken, poached and cooled in its cooking liquid

1½ to 2 cups Mayonnaise (see page 36)

Salt and freshly milled white pepper

4 carrots, peeled and cut into julienne

3 parsnips, peeled and cut into julienne

1 small celery root (celeriac), peeled and cut into julienne

1 small rutabaga, peeled and cut into ½-inch julienne

2 small pears, thinly sliced from stem to base (including the stem)

1 bunch white icicle radishes, peeled, thinly sliced lengthwise, and reserved in ice water

4 Jerusalem artichokes, peeled, thinly sliced, and reserved in ice water

¼ cup chopped Italian parsley

Vinaigrette (see page 35)

Salt and freshly milled black pepper

Method

When the chicken is cool enough to handle, pull all of the meat off the bones and return the bones and skin to the stock. Boil the stock over high heat for 45 minutes to reduce and enrich it.

Meanwhile, cut the chicken into ¾-inch cubes. Cover and chill.

When the chicken is cold, fold in enough of the mayonnaise to coat lightly. Season with salt and white pepper to taste. (The chicken salad can be made a day ahead.)

Strain the stock; discard the solids. Return the liquids to the pot and bring the stock to a simmer.

Stir in a small amount of salt. Add the carrots and simmer until just tender. Remove with a slotted spoon; drain and set aside.

Add the parsnips and simmer until just tender; remove, drain, and set aside. Continue as before, cooking the celery root, rutabaga, and pears until just tender. Reserve stock for another use.

Drain the radishes and the Jerusalem artichokes. Pat dry with paper towels.

In a large bowl, combine all of the vegetables, the pears, and the parsley. Add the vinaigrette and toss to coat. Season with salt and black pepper to taste.

To serve, spoon the vegetables on 4 or 5 dinner plates. Spoon the chicken salad over the vegetables.

Serves 4 to 5

Calories: for 4—1,320 per serving
for 5—1,060 per serving (using ¼ cup vinaigrette and 1½ cup mayonnaise)

Wine: Chardonnay

SMOKED CHICKEN AND WILD RICE SALAD

The lusty tart fruits and nutty wild rice are the perfect foil for the smoky-flavored chicken in this salad. It can be served at room temperature or the bird can be warmed slightly and then added to this rich dish.

Ingredients

2½ to 3-pound smoked chicken

1 cup wild rice, washed thoroughly in several changes of cold water

2 cups chicken stock or broth

1 bunch scallions

1 tablespoon unsalted butter

1 cup walnut pieces

1 tablespoon grainy mustard

1 garlic clove, minced

Salt and freshly milled black pepper

¼ cup sherry vinegar

Juice of ½ orange

½ cup vegetable oil

¼ cup Oriental sesame oil

A few dashes of hot pepper oil (see page 27)

16 kumquats, halved and seeds removed if large

1 cup fresh cranberries, washed and drained

Method

Skin the chicken and pull the meat off the bones in thin shreds.

In a large saucepan, combine the wild rice, stock, and enough cold water to cover by 1 inch. Bring to a boil over moderate heat. Boil for 25 to 30 minutes, until tender. Drain and reserve.

Meanwhile, trim the scallions at both ends. Cut them into long thin strips. Place in a bowl of ice water.

In a small skillet, melt the butter over moderate heat. When the foam subsides, add the walnuts and toast, shaking the pan, until golden. Drain on paper towels.

In a bowl, whisk together the mustard, garlic, and salt and pepper to taste. Whisk in the vinegar and orange juice until the salt dissolves. Gradually whisk in the oils; set the dressing aside.

In a large mixing bowl, combine the chicken, wild rice, kumquats, and cranberries. Toss to coat with the dressing. Set aside at room temperature for 30 minutes.

Drain the scallions.

Divide the salad among 4 or 5 dinner plates. Scatter with the scallions and walnuts and serve.

Serves 4 to 5

Calories: for 4—910 per serving
for 5—729 per serving

Wine: Chianti

PINEAPPLE, RED CABBAGE, AND SMOKED HOCK SALAD

Pineapples are a dependable winter fruit, and cabbage is with us year round. The addition of the smoked ham hock is an inexpensive way of making something special out of nothing. If you don't have a crock of brandied cherries, buy the dried red ones from Michigan and soak them in brandy until plumped.

Ingredients

1 small red cabbage, trimmed, cored, quartered, and cut into thin strips

3 smoked ham hocks

1 celery rib, coarsely chopped

½ cinnamon stick

4 whole cloves

6 black peppercorns

1 bay leaf

1 small onion, halved

1 small pineapple, peeled, quartered lengthwise, cored, and cut into ⅓-inch slices

1 red bell pepper, seeded, deveined, and cut into julienne

¼ cup brandied black baby cherries, drained

Dressing

1 tablespoon honey mustard

Salt and freshly milled white pepper

⅓ cup raspberry vinegar (see page 31)

½ cup safflower or vegetable oil

1 tablespoon Oriental sesame oil

Method

In a large pot of lightly salted boiling water, blanch the cabbage for 30 seconds. Drain and reserve in the colander.

In a medium saucepan, combine the ham hocks with the celery, cinnamon, cloves, peppercorns, bay leaf, and onion. Add cold water to cover by 1 inch. Bring to a boil over high heat. Reduce the heat and simmer until the hocks are tender, about 40 minutes. Drain and reserve only the ham hocks. Set aside to cool.

When the hocks are cool, pull off all the meat; discard the fat, skin, and bones.

In a large bowl, toss together the cabbage, ham, pineapple, bell pepper, and cherries.

In a nonreactive small saucepan, combine all of the dressing ingredients and bring to a simmer over moderate heat.

Pour the dressing over the salad. Toss thoroughly and serve.

Serves 3 to 4

Calories: for 3—670 per serving
for 4—505 per serving

Wine: Jekel (Monterey) or Kabinett Riesling

BOILED BEEF WITH ROOT VEGETABLES AND HORSERADISH SAUCE

Boiled beef is usually best when it comes hot from the pot. It does not reheat well and usually winds up between slices of rye bread. This is an extender meal that uses up the leftovers and becomes festive.

Ingredients

1 pound boiled beef, with all fat removed

1 small celery root (celeriac), peeled and cut into long ½-inch julienne

3 parsnips, peeled and cut into long ½-inch julienne

3 carrots, peeled and cut into long ½-inch julienne

2 firm but ripe pears, peeled, cored, and cut into ½-inch julienne

Juice of ½ lemon

2 tablespoons chopped parsley

¾ cup Vinaigrette (see page 35)

Salt and freshly milled black pepper

Sauce

1 tablespoon freshly grated horseradish

1 tablespoon drained chopped capers

2 tablespoons chopped dill

½ cup sour cream

⅓ cup heavy cream, whipped

Salt and freshly milled white pepper

Method

Cut the beef into thin slices. Cover and refrigerate.

In a pan of lightly salted boiling water, cook the vegetables, one at a time, until just crisp-tender. Remove each type with a slotted spoon and set aside to cool.

Toss the pear julienne with the lemon juice. Cover and set aside.

In a large bowl, combine the vegetables, pears, parsley, and enough of the vinaigrette to coat lightly. Toss gently and season with salt and black pepper to taste. Cover and refrigerate.

In a small bowl, combine the horseradish, capers, and dill. Fold in the sour cream and whipped cream; season with salt and white pepper to taste. Cover and refrigerate.

To serve, toss the beef with the vegetables. Divide among 4 dinner plates. Pass the horseradish sauce separately.

Serves 4

Calories: salad—590 per serving
sauce—33 per tablespoon

Wine: Côtes du Rhône or Jos. Phelps Syrah

BRAISED SWEETBREADS, QUAIL EGGS, AND MACHE SALAD

Sweetbreads are rich and full of calories and cholesterol, but the fancier of these tender, buttery meats really does not care. Here, they are lightened up with fluffy clusters of *mâche* and punctuated with sweet pickled beets and tart capers.

Ingredients

1 pair medium veal sweetbreads, about 16 ounces

2 tablespoons unsalted butter

1 small onion, chopped

1 celery rib, chopped

1 carrot, chopped

1 cup dry white wine

1 sprig fresh thyme

1 sprig fresh rosemary

⅓ cup fresh lemon juice

1 tablespoon honey mustard

Salt and cayenne pepper

⅓ cup walnut oil

⅔ cup vegetable oil

2 tablespoons heavy cream

8 ounces *mâche* (about 8 handfuls), washed and trimmed, but left in clusters

4 medium pickled beets

12 quail eggs, hard-cooked, peeled, and halved lengthwise

2 tablespoons capers, washed and drained

Method

Wash the sweetbreads. Place in a bowl of ice water and set aside for 45 minutes.

Drain the sweetbreads and place them in a pot of lightly salted water. Bring the water to a simmer and cook for 10 minutes. Drain and cool under cold running water.

Carefully remove the outer membrane and any fatty tissue from the sweetbreads.

Place the sweetbreads on a paper towel-lined plate, cover with another plate, and weigh down with a heavy object or can. Refrigerate for 2 hours. (This cleaning process can be done as much as a day ahead.)

In a medium skillet, melt the butter over moderate heat. Add the chopped vegetables and cook until the onion wilts. Add the wine and bring to a simmer.

Place the sweetbreads and herbs on top of the vegetables. Cover partially and "steam" the sweetbreads for about 20 minutes.

Meanwhile, make the dressing. In a medium bowl, whisk together the lemon juice, mustard, and salt and cayenne to taste. Gradually add the oils, whisking until emulsified. Whisk in the cream.

Toss the *mâche* with about half of the dressing. Mound the *mâche* on a large platter. Arrange the beets and quail eggs over the greens.

When the sweetbreads are cooked, cut them into ⅓-inch slices. Arrange over the *mâche*. Spoon the remaining dressing over the sweetbreads and sprinkle with the capers.

Serves 4

Calories: 830 per serving

Wine: Full-bodied Chardonnay

For a brief time around Christmas summer fruits from the southern hemisphere arrive in our markets. Plums, peaches, melons, and other summer reminders can be delicious. If grilling food for a main course dinner, then certainly prepare this fruit dessert for the grill. Otherwise, use the broiler, or even a toaster oven will do.

Ingredients

½ small winter melon

1 persimmon

2 to 3 medium pears

Juice of 2 lemons

2 peaches

1 mango

2 cups strawberry preserves

2 tablespoons kirsch

Method

You will need 16 long wooden skewers for this recipe. Soak them in water.

Peel and seed the melon. Cut the flesh into 2-inch cubes; set aside.

Peel the persimmon. Cut into 2-inch chunks; set aside.

Quarter the pears lengthwise, leaving the cores and stem intact. Brush with some of the lemon juice to prevent them from browning.

Blanch and peel the peaches. Cut into quarters and brush with some of the lemon juice.

Peel the mango. Cut into long crescent slices about 1 inch wide.

Preheat the broiler or prepare a charcoal fire.

In a heavy saucepan or double broiler, combine the preserves and kirsch. Melt together over low heat.

Skewer the fruits, starting with the melon and ending with the peaches and mango.

If using the broiler, set the skewers on a lightly oiled baking sheet. Toast, turning once, just until the fruits begin to give off their juices.

If grilling the kebabs, oil the grill lightly. When the coals are ash-covered and glowing, set the skewers on the rack and quickly sear the fruits until lightly charred.

Place a spoonful or two of the warm preserves on each plate and arrange 4 skewers over the sauce.

Serves 4

Calories: fruit—150 per serving
sauce—50 per tablespoon

Wine: Pink Champagne

SMOKED FISH SALAD

Smoked store-bought fish such as salmon and sturgeon are readily available to all of us. But home-smoked fish is another taste entirely. Fish, such as blues, cod, and eels, and shellfish, such as oysters, scallops, and mussels, can be cold- or hot-smoked at home, and one can dine well on these delicious creatures. The small smokers are inexpensive and simple to use.

Ingredients

4- to 5-pounds (1 side) hot-smoked salmon (Northwest Indian cure or East Coast fruit-wood cure)

4 to 6 sides smoked bluefish (about 4 pounds)

3 smoked eels (about 2 pounds)

2 pounds smoked scallops

12 large Belgian endives

1½ cups Vinaigrette (see page 35)

2 cups Mayonnaise (see page 36)

¼ cup chopped parsley

3 tablespoons chopped chives, or 4 scallions, trimmed and chopped, including some of the green

3 tablespoons chopped dill

6 lemons, cut into wedges

1 cup freshly grated horseradish

Method

Cut the slab of salmon into ½-inch slices as you would slice a ham. Cut the bluefish into ½-inch slices. Cut the eel into ½-inch slices.

Arrange all of the smoked fish and shellfish on a large serving platter. Refrigerate. Remove 20 minutes before serving.

Core the endives and cut crosswise in half. Cut each half lengthwise into long julienne.

Toss the endive with enough of the vinaigrette to just coat it lightly. Cover and refrigerate.

Make the mayonnaise and fold in the parsley, chives, and dill until the color is dark green.
Cover and refrigerate.

Serve the fish salad with the endive salad, herbed mayonnaise, lemon wedges and horseradish. Serve with hot buttered toast or dark bread.

Serves 12

Calories: fish—868 per serving
endive salad—160 per serving
mayonnaise—130 per tablespoon
horseradish—6 per tablespoon

Wine: Fumé Blanc or Aquavit

FRESH TUNA AND BROCCOLI SALAD

The ubiquitous broccoli is winter's sturdy vegetable. Here it is incorporated into an unusual *Niçoise* with cooked fresh tuna fish.

Ingredients

1- to 1¼-pound fresh tuna steak, cut 1 inch thick

2 sprigs fresh rosemary, or 1 teaspoon dried

2 sprigs fresh thyme, or 1 teaspoon dried

Small bunch garlic chives or chives

1 bay leaf

2 garlic cloves

6 to 8 black peppercorns

About 2¼ cups olive oil

1 head broccoli, trimmed and cut into florets

2 large pimientos or 1 large red pepper, roasted peeled, seeded, and cut into fine dice

½ cup *Niçoise* olives

Juice and grated zest of 1 lemon

Coarse (kosher) salt and freshly milled black pepper

Method

Preheat the oven to 225 degrees.

Place the fish in an ovenproof dish that will hold it tightly.

Pack in the herbs, garlic, and peppercorns. Pour in enough of the olive oil to cover completely.

Cover the dish with foil; set in a baking pan and pour in boiling water to reach halfway up the sides of the dish.

Bake for 1 hour, or until the tuna easily can be pierced with the tip of a knife. Remove from the oven to cool.

Remove the fish from the oil and flake it with a fork. (Reserve the oil for another use.)

Steam the broccoli until crisp-tender. Cool under running water; drain and set aside.

To serve the salad, toss together the tuna, broccoli, pimientos, olives, lemon juice, lemon zest, and about ¼ cup olive oil. Season with salt and pepper to taste. Serve at room temperature.

Serves 4

Calories: 490 per serving

Wine: Rioja

RED BEANS WITH SHRIMP

Kidney beans are a versatile legume and one of my favorites. Combined with juicy shrimp, they make a quirky but tasty salad.

Ingredients

8 ounces dried kidney beans, or 1 can (15 ounces) kidney beans, washed and drained

½ lemon, sliced

1 tablespoon dried red pepper flakes

16 to 18 medium-large shrimp, in their shells

¼ cup olive oil

2 tablespoons white wine vinegar

2 garlic cloves, minced

2 tablespoons chopped Italian parsley

Salt

1 small bunch chicory, washed and dried

Method

Pick over the beans and rinse well. Place in a saucepan with salted water to cover and bring to a boil. Reduce the heat and simmer for 1 hour, or until tender. Drain and reserve. (If using canned beans, drain and set aside.)

In a pot of lightly salted boiling water, combine the lemon slices, half of the red pepper flakes, and the shrimp. Bring back to a boil and cook for 2 minutes. Drain and place the shrimp in a bowl of ice.

When cool, peel and devein the shrimp, leaving the tail intact.

In a bowl, whisk together the oil and vinegar. Add the beans and toss. Stir in the remaining red pepper flakes, the garlic, and parsley. Stir in the shrimp and toss. Season with salt to taste.

Divide the chicory between 2 dinner plates. Spoon the salad over the greens and serve.

Serves 2

Calories: 700 per serving

Wine: Provençal or California (Simi) Rosé

STEAMED FISH SALAD

The ingredients in this salad add zest and flavor to sole—a pale fish that demands embellishment.

Ingredients

2 bunches scallions

2 tablespoons fresh lemon juice

1 tablespoon fresh orange juice

1 garlic clove, minced

Salt and freshly milled white pepper

3 tablespoons peanut oil

1 tablespoon hot pepper oil

2 bunches broccoli raab, washed and trimmed

3 strips orange zest, cut into fine dice

1 large yellow bell pepper, cored, deveined, and cut into fine julienne

4 ounces *enoki* mushrooms, trimmed

4 fillets of sole, preferably lemon or gray sole (about 1¾ pounds)

Method

Trim the scallions and cut them into 3-inch lengths. Finely slice into one end several times, cutting only about ¾-inch deep. Turn the scallion around and cut the other end in the same way to make scallion "brushes." Place in a bowl of ice water so that the cut ends curl.

In a small bowl, whisk the lemon and orange juices with the garlic and salt and pepper to taste. Whisk in the oils; set the dressing aside.

Place the broccoli raab in a large steamer and cook for 5 minutes.

Sprinkle with the orange zest and add the bell pepper julienne. Cook for 3 minutes.

Place the scallion brushes on one side of the steamer and the mushrooms on the other side. Cover the broccoli raab with the fish fillets. Steam for 3 minutes, or until the fish is opaque but not flaky.

Place a fish fillet on each of 4 heated dinner plates. Arrange the vegetables around the fish. Spoon some of the dressing over each fillet. Serve at once, while warm.

Serves 4

Calories: 325 per serving

Wine: Mâcon-Villages

SALMON CRAB CAKES WITH EXOTIC FRUITS AND GREENS

Every winter season new and exotic fruits are introduced to us from around the globe. This zesty and brightly colorful salad combines some of the more exotic fruits we find at good produce markets—the ones we stare at, wondering how to use them.

Ingredients

Fish Cakes

8 ounces cooked leftover salmon or fresh salmon

8 ounces lump crabmeat, picked over

3 scallions, minced (including some of the green)

1 tablespoon chopped parsley

⅛ teaspoon freshly grated nutmeg

¼ teaspoon Old Bay Seasoning

¼ cup cracker meal

¼ cup Mayonnaise (see page 36)

1 teaspoon Dijon mustard

1 egg, beaten

Cracker meal, for dredging

Vegetable oil, for frying

Sauce

½ cup plain yogurt

½ cup Mayonnaise (see page 36)

1 tablespoon drained chopped capers, dried

1 tablespoon minced cilantro

¼ cup chopped papaya

Salad

1 tablespoon unsalted butter

1 hot red cherry pepper, seeded, deveined, and cut into fine julienne

1 semi-ripe papaya, peeled, seeded, and cut into ½-inch dice

2 persimmons, peeled and cut into ½-inch strips

3 ears fresh sweet corn, cut off the cobs, or ¾ cup frozen corn kernels, thawed

1 bunch watercress, trimmed, washed, and dried

1 bunch arugula, trimmed, washed, and dried

1 large head radicchio, washed, dried, and cut into ½-inch strips

1 tablespoon chopped cilantro

⅓ cup fruity olive oil

Salt and freshly milled black pepper

Juice and seeds of 2 small pomegranates

3 tamarillos, peeled, halved, and cut into eighths

Method

Make the cakes: If using fresh salmon, steam it for 4 minutes.

In a bowl, combine the salmon, crabmeat, scallions, parsley, nutmeg, Old Bay Seasoning, cracker meal, mayonnaise, mustard, and egg. Mix very well. Cover and refrigerate for at least 1 hour.

Shape the cold mixture into 8 small cakes. Coat very well in cracker crumbs. Place on a plate and refrigerate for at least 1 hour.

Pour ¼ inch of vegetable oil into a large skillet; set aside for frying the cakes.

To make the sauce, combine all of the sauce ingredients in a bowl.

Cover and refrigerate until serving time.

To make the salad, melt the butter in a medium skillet over moderate heat.

Add the cherry pepper and cook until wilted. Add the papaya and persimmons and cook until they begin to "sweat."

Stir in the corn and cook until heated through. Set aside and keep warm.

In a large bowl, combine all of the greens with the cilantro. Toss with the olive oil. Season with salt and pepper to taste. Sprinkle with the pomegranate juice and seeds and the tamarillos.

Place the skillet and vegetable oil over moderate heat. When the oil is hot, add the fish cakes and fry, turning as necessary, until browned on all sides.

To serve, divide the greens, vegetables, and fruit among 4 dinner plates. Place 2 fish cakes on each plate and pass the sauce separately.

Serves 4

Calories: 875 per serving
sauce: 290 per serving

Wine: Dry rosé

PRAWN AND AVOCADO SALAD

This quick and easy dish plays on soft and crisp textures and flavors that are sweet, tart, and hot. The Jerusalem artichoke (also called sunchoke) is tasty whether cooked or raw.

Ingredients

10 to 12 jumbo shrimp or prawns, in their shells

¼ cup plus 2 tablespoons olive oil

2 garlic cloves, slivered

1 tablespoon chopped cilantro

1 teaspoon dried red pepper flakes

Juice of 1½ lemons

2 small ripe avocados

1 grapefruit, sectioned

1 Jerusalem artichoke, peeled

Method

In a bowl, combine the shrimp, ¼ cup of the olive oil, the garlic, cilantro, red pepper flakes, and one-third of the lemon juice. Cover and set aside for 1 hour.

Peel and pit the avocados. Cut into long thin crescents and place in a bowl. Sprinkle with half of the remaining lemon juice. Cover and set aside.

Remove the shrimp from the marinade.

In a large skillet, heat the remaining 2 tablespoons oil over high heat. When almost smoking, add the shrimp and cook very fast until they begin to char, about 4 minutes.

Divide the grapefruit and avocado slices between 2 dinner plates. Spoon the shrimp over them. Grate the Jerusalem artichoke over each plate and sprinkle with the remaining lemon juice. Serve at once.

Serves 2

Calories: 705 per serving (using ¼ cup oil)

Wine: Chilled sherry

STONE CRAB SALAD

Stone crabs are one of Florida's treats from November until April. Their tough-shelled claws are usually served up on a bowl of ice, with mallets, crackers, and pickers for extracting the meat before dipping it into a hot mustardy mayonnaise. Here, you have done all the work for your guests.

Ingredients

3 pounds stone crabclaws; picked clean (8–10 ounces)

½ cup Mayonnaise (see page 36), with 1 teaspoon Coleman's dry mustard added

8 ounces snow peas, trimmed

½ lotus root, peeled and sliced paper-thin

1 small jicama, peeled, sliced, and cut into julienne

2 tablespoons plum wine vinegar, or 1 tablespoon plum wine mixed with 1 tablespoon rice wine vinegar

¼ cup peanut oil

Salt and freshly milled white pepper

Grated zest of ½ lemon

Method

Place the crab in a bowl and stir in enough of the mayonnaise to coat it well. Cover and refrigerate.

Steam the snow peas until crisp-tender. Cool under cold running water and drain well.

In a large mixing bowl, combine the snow peas, lotus root, and jicama. Sprinkle on the vinegar and toss. Add the oil and toss again. Season with salt and pepper to taste.

Divide the vegetables between 2 dinner plates.

Spoon the chilled crab salad over the vegetables and scatter the lemon zest on top.

Serves 2

Calories: 1,061 per serving

Wine: Sauvignon Blanc (Arbor Crest)

SCALLOPS AND CINNABAR MELON

Scallops from the sea or bay should never be overcooked. For this recipe, the fruit should be perfectly ripe, and all the ingredients then require is a brief sauté. If cinnabar melon is not available, substitute papaya.

Ingredients

4 tablespoons light olive oil

1 cinnabar melon, halved, peeled, seeded, and cut into ½-inch cubes

1 small medium-hot pepper, halved, seeded, and cut into fine julienne

2 carambolas (star fruits), cut into ⅓-inch slices (remove the brown)

1 pound bay or sea scallops

⅓ cup raspberry or other fruit vinegar (see page 31)

Salt and freshly milled white pepper

2 bunches *mâche,* washed and trimmed, but left in small clusters

Method

In a medium nonstick skillet, heat 2 tablespoons of the oil over moderately low heat. Add the melon, pepper, and carambolas and tightly cover. Cook for 4 minutes, or until the fruit begins to "sweat."

Add the scallops and cover the skillet. Cook for 3 to 4 minutes, or until the scallops are opaque.

Remove from the heat. Using a slotted spoon, divide the ingredients to the *side* of 4 dinner plates.

Return the skillet to moderate heat and add the remaining 2 tablespoons olive oil. Bring to a boil and stir in the vinegar. Season the dressing with salt and pepper to taste.

Remove from the heat and add the *mâche* to the dressing. Toss lightly and divide among the dinner plates. Serve at once.

Serves 4

Calories: 345 per serving

Wine: California or Alsatian Gewürztraminer

SAUTEED PRAWN SALAD

This Italianate salad is redolent with the lusty flavors of the Mediterranean. The dill, an herb rarely used in France and virtually not at all in Italy, is my addition because it works so well.

Ingredients

12 baby artichokes, trimmed

2 tablespoons olive oil

8 garlic cloves, peeled but left whole

2 to 3 large yellow bell peppers, seeded, deveined, and cut into julienne

2 hot red chile peppers, seeded, deveined, and cut into julienne

12 large raw prawns or shrimp, peeled and deveined, with tail intact

1 small head white chicory or *frisée,* washed and dried

½ cup Vinaigrette (see page 35)

2 tablespoons chopped dill

Method

Cook the artichokes in salted boiling water until almost tender, about 5 minutes. Cool under cold running water; drain and reserve.

In a large skillet over moderate heat, combine the oil, garlic, and peppers. Cook until the peppers wilt, 3 to 4 minutes.

Remove the peppers with tongs and set aside. Add the artichokes to the skillet and toss in the oil.

Add the shrimp and cook until tender, about 4 minutes. Remove and reserve.

Continue cooking the garlic until golden. Remove and reserve.

Toss the chicory with the vinaigrette; divide among 3 or 4 dinner plates.

Divide the vegetables, shrimp, and garlic among the plates. Sprinkle each portion with some of the dill and serve.

Serves 3 to 4

Calories: for 3—550 per serving
for 4—415 per serving

Wine: Italian Tocai

SEARED SALMON, MACHE, AND MARINATED ONION SALAD

The natural juices and oil in salmon makes it ideal for a quick sear that requires no additional fat. The balsamic vinegar is available in many vintages. I suggest using the oldest and most expensive you can afford.

Ingredients

About ⅓ cup aged balsamic vinegar

Salt and freshly milled black pepper

1 medium red onion, thinly sliced from stem to root

2 to 3 tablespoons olive oil

8 ounces Rome mushrooms or white mushrooms, cleaned and sliced ¼ inch thick

8 to 12 ounces skinless boneless fresh salmon fillet, thinly sliced

4 ounces *mâche,* washed and trimmed, but left in clusters

1 small head radicchio, washed and cut into chiffonade

Method

In a small nonreactive saucepan, heat the vinegar until wisps of steam rise from the surface. Sprinkle on salt and pepper to taste. Add the onion slices; set aside.

In a small skillet, heat enough of the oil to lightly coat the bottom of the pan. Add the mushrooms and sprinkle with salt and pepper. Sauté briefly, or just until the mushrooms begin to give off their liquid. Remove and reserve.

In a nonstick skillet over moderate heat, sear the salmon quickly, turning once. Remove to a plate and keep warm. Strain the onions, reserving their vinegar.

In a bowl, toss the *mâche,* radicchio, the mushrooms and their juices, and 2 tablespoons of the reserved onion vinegar. Stir in 1 tablespoon oil. Season with salt and pepper to taste.

Divide the salad between 2 warm dinner plates. Divide the salmon and steeped onions over the greens. Serve at once.

Serves 2

Calories: 450 per serving (using 8 ounces of salmon) 539 per serving (using 12 ounces of salmon)

Wine: Chilean Sauvignon Blanc or Cabernet Sauvignon

JOHN HAESSLER'S PICKLED HERRING

Man has been known to survive on salted and pickled herring. On a cold winter's night nothing is more satisfying than a dish of this put-up fish with a plate of boiled potatoes and an iced beer.

Ingredients

1¼ pounds table salt (1⅔ cup)

2 pounds herring fillets with skin (see Note), cut into 2-inch chunks

2 tablespoons pickling spices

1 cup sugar

3 cups distilled white vinegar

1 green bell pepper, seeded and sliced

1 red bell pepper, seeded and sliced

1 medium white onion, sliced

1 medium red onion, sliced

2 tablespoons chopped dill

Method

In a large nonreactive kettle or basin combine the salt with 1 gallon of water. Stir well and allow to sit until the salt dissolves.

Wash the fillets in cold water. Add to the brine and set aside for 45 minutes.

Drain the fish in a colander.

Meanwhile, in a nonreactive medium saucepan, combine the pickling spices, sugar, and vinegar. Bring to a boil over high heat, stirring until the sugar dissolves.

Remove from the heat; set aside to cool to room temperature.

When cool, add the vegetables and dill. Add the fish fillets. Cover and refrigerate for 3 to 4 days (see Note), stirring from time to time.

Pack the herring and vegetables in sterilized jars and fill with the pickling liquid. Refrigerate for up to 3 weeks.

Serves 6 to 8

Calories: for 6—338 per serving
for 8—253 per serving

Beverage: beer or Aquavit

Note: Blue herring is best for pickling as are mackerel, bluefish, or any firm-fleshed white fish. Pickling time depends on the thickness of the fish.

SWEDISH BEET SALAD

Ingredients

4 medium beets, cooked, thinly sliced, and cut into julienne

Juice of ½ lemon

¼ teaspoon caraway seed

Salt and freshly milled white pepper

½ cup heavy cream, whipped, or ½ cup *crème fraîche*

2 strips orange zest, cut into needle-thin julienne and chopped very fine

Method

In a mixing bowl, combine the beet julienne, lemon juice, and caraway seed. Toss well; season with salt and pepper to taste. Cover and chill for 2 hours.

Fold in the cream and half of the orange zest. Cover and refrigerate until chilled.

To serve, mound in a serving bowl and sprinkle the remaining zest over the salad.

Serves 4

Calories: 125 per serving

HOT POTATO SALAD WITH DILL

Ingredients

2 dozen very small red or new potatoes

⅓ cup olive oil

2 tablespoons chopped dill

2 strips lemon zest, cut into needle-thin julienne and chopped very fine

Salt and freshly milled white pepper

Method

Preheat the oven to 225 degrees.

Pare the potatoes into 2-inch olive shapes.

In a pot of lightly salted boiling water, cook the potatoes until tender. Drain and keep warm.

Place the potatoes in a mixing bowl. Add the oil, dill, and lemon zest and toss gently. Season with salt and pepper to taste.

Place in a serving bowl and serve along with the pickled herring and beet salad.

Serves 4 to 6

Calories: for 4—375 per serving
for 6—250 per serving

The most humble of winter's choices can be elevated to a dish that is tasty and exquisite. Pairing bacon and fish is an old New England custom. Though regular walnuts can be substituted for the black ones, black walnuts are a richer, more buttery, treat.

Ingredients

½ small white cabbage, cored and sliced ½ inch thick

3 slices smoked bacon, cut into ½-inch squares

½ cup black walnut pieces

¼ cup Champagne vinegar

¼ cup heavy cream

8 ounces fresh scrod or codfish fillets, cut into 1-inch cubes

Freshly milled white pepper

Method

In a pot of lightly salted boiling water, blanch the cabbage for 1 minute. Drain in a colander; reserve.

In a nonreactive heavy skillet, fry the bacon pieces over low heat until golden. Drain on paper towels.

Reserving 1 tablespoon of the bacon fat, pour out most of the remaining fat, leaving just a thin film in the skillet.

Add the nuts and toast over low heat. Remove with a slotted spoon; drain on paper towels.

Add the vinegar to the skillet and boil over high heat until reduced to a glaze.

Add the cream and cabbage and toss to coat it. Cook until heated through, about 5 minutes.

Meanwhile, pour the reserved bacon fat into a large nonstick skillet and place over moderate heat. When hot, add the fish and cook for 3 to 4 minutes, turning once, until opaque.

Toss the lardons and the toasted nuts with the cabbage. Divide between 2 warmed plates. Add the fish pieces and serve at once.

Serves 2

Calories: 670 per serving

Wine: Alsatian dry white wine

DANDELION AND WILD ONION SALAD

Come spring, we want the freshness and flavor of something new and green and grown very close to nature. Dandelion greens herald the newness and satisfy that hankering—totally.

Ingredients

1 pound dandelion greens, with roots and buds included (see Note)

24 wild onion roots (see Note)

6 slices thick-cut bacon, cut crosswise into ½-inch strips

1½ cups beef stock

2 tablespoons Dijon mustard

2 tablespoons cider vinegar

Salt and freshly milled black pepper

24 fresh violets, stems removed, or the petals of 2 dandelion flowers

Method

Wash the greens and onion pips thoroughly. Remove the roots, leaving the dandelion greens in full clusters. Wash the greens two more times to remove all grit. Spin dry; refrigerate.

In a nonreactive skillet over moderate heat, render the bacon until golden. Drain on paper towels.

Pour the bacon fat out of the skillet. Add the stock and stir in the mustard, vinegar, and salt and pepper to taste.

Simmer the stock mixture over moderate heat for about 6 minutes.

Add the onion pips and cook for 4 minutes. Continue cooking as necessary until the sauce is reduced to about 1 cup.

Meanwhile, place the greens in a glass or ceramic bowl.

Pour the sauce over the greens. Sprinkle with the bacon and mix well.

Sprinkle the violets over the salad. Serve with toasted crusty garlic bread.

Serves 4

Calories: 230 per serving

Wine: Pinot Bianco

Note: The greens should be picked during the last 2 to 3 weeks of April, depending on the spring weather, or otherwise the dandelion becomes bitter and prickly and the onion bulbs woody. The tiny caper-like bud of the dandelion can be dusted with flour and fried in bacon fat for a nutty, crunchy flavor and texture.

MESCLUN SALAD

It is the freshness of this salad that appeals—a prelude to the bounty of summer—and keeps us content until the first perfect tomato in August.

Ingredients

12 ounces sweet and tender salad greens, such as loose-leaf, butterhead, or oak leaf lettuce, spinach, young beet leaves, or young turnip greens

6 ounces sharp and peppery salad greens, such as dandelion, arugula, field cress, baby curly endive, or baby mustard greens

1 cup very loosely packed chervil and parsley sprigs

⅓ cup light fruit vinegar (see page 31)

1 teaspoon sugar

⅓ cup light olive oil

⅓ cup vegetable oil

Salt and freshly milled white pepper

½ cup herb blossoms, such as chervil, thyme, or rosemary mixed with nasturtiums or *rosa rugosa* petals

Method

Wash and spin dry all of the greens and herb sprigs. Chill until serving time.

In a small nonreactive saucepan, warm the vinegar and sugar over moderate heat until the sugar dissolves. Set aside to cool.

Whisk the oils into the sweetened vinegar. Season with salt and pepper to taste.

In a large bowl, toss the greens and herbs with enough of the dressing to coat lightly. Divide among 4 chilled plates.

Sprinkle the salads with the blossoms and petals and serve. Accompany with lightly toasted thick slices of crusty Italian bread and any triple-crème cheese or Gorgonzola and Mascarpone torta.

Serves 4

Calories: 260 per serving (using ⅔ of dressing to coat)

Wine: Dry rosé or Black Muscat

ABOUT THE AUTHOR

Christopher Idone is one of New York's most respected and admired culinary artists. In 1971 he cofounded the world-famous catering organization, Glorious Food, Inc., and left ten years later to begin work on his first cookbook. The pioneering Glorious Food (1982) became an immediate best seller and was followed by the award-winning Glorious American Food (1985). Salad Days is his third book.

Mr. Idone is a frequent contributor to The New York Times Magazine and to other publications. He is also designer of the Millefiore dinnerware collection, and a food consultant and lecturer.

GRAPHIC CREDITS

The color separations in this book were prepared by Tien Wah Press, Singapore, from original photographs by Christopher Idone.

The text was composed in film by Graphic Composition, Athens, Georgia.

The book was printed and bound by Tien Wah Press, Singapore.

R. D. Scudellari designed and directed the graphics.